THE

&

SCIENCE
OF MONEY
LAUNDERING

Inside the Commerce of the
International Narcotics Traffickers

Brett F. Woods

PALADIN PRESS · BOULDER, COLORADO

THE 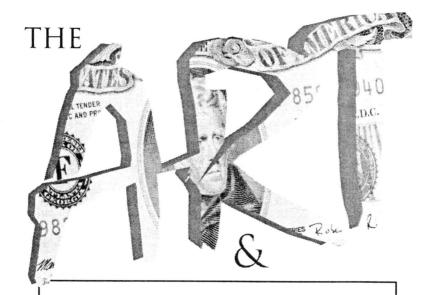 &

SCIENCE
OF MONEY
LAUNDERING

The Art and Science of Money Laundering:
Inside the Commerce of International Narcotics Trafficking
by Brett F. Woods

Copyright © 1998 by Brett F. Woods

ISBN 0-87364-969-6
Printed in the United States of America

Published by Paladin Press, a division of
Paladin Enterprises, Inc., P.O. Box 1307,
Boulder, Colorado 80306, USA.
(303) 443-7250

Direct inquiries and/or orders to the above address.

PALADIN, PALADIN PRESS, and the "horse head" design
are trademarks belonging to Paladin Enterprises and
registered in United States Patent and Trademark Office.

CONTENTS

Financial Intelligence Units
Training and Technical Assistance
Significant Enforcement Cases
Asset Sharing
Representative Financial Action Task Force Activities
The Summit of the Americas

AUTHOR'S NOTE

The information presented in this monograph is drawn from open source material, viewpoints, and other documents provided by the U.S. Department of Justice, U.S. Department of State, U.S. Department of the Treasury, U.S. Treasury Financial Crimes Enforcement Network, and the U.S. General Accounting Office. Any conclusions drawn herein are solely the responsibility of the author and should not be interpreted as official policy statements of the U.S. government.

Brett F. Woods
Santa Fe, New Mexico

INTRODUCTION

The Money-Laundering Phenomenon

Money laundering is the disguising or concealing of illicit income to make the income appear legitimate. Federal law enforcement officials estimate that between $100 and $300 billion in U.S. currency is laundered each year. While narcotics traffickers are by far the largest single block of users of money-laundering schemes, numerous other types of activities typical of organized crime (e.g., illegal gambling, prostitution) also create an appreciable demand for what has become nothing less than an art form.

Although the process of money laundering has been broken down into any number of steps, it is generally agreed by law enforcement and regulatory officials that the point at which criminals are most vulnerable to detection is *placement*, the concealing of illicit proceeds by (1) converting the cash to another medium that is more convenient or less suspicious for purposes of exchange, such as property, cashier's checks, or money orders, or (2) depositing the funds into a financial institution account for subsequent disbursement.

Because of the problems associated with converting and concealing large amounts of cash, placement is perhaps the most difficult part of money laundering. Consequently, this vulnerability is exploited and is the primary focus of U.S. law enforcement, legislative, and regulatory efforts to attack money laundering.

Financial institutions are in a unique position to assist law enforcement at the federal and state levels by reporting suspicious transactions that might indicate money laundering. Reports of suspicious transactions have initiated a number of major investigations into a wide range of criminal activity.

However, given the lack of overall direction and control of reporting suspicious transactions, reports filed with different agencies on different forms vary as to the amount of useful information they contain. Although the Internal Revenue Service (IRS) has successfully used the reports to initiate a number of investigations, the management of—and emphasis given to—the information varies among IRS district offices. To date, the IRS has no agency-wide policies or procedures on how best to solicit, process, and use the information. Because the IRS cannot be certain that the information is used and managed consistently, it has no assurance that the information is used to its full potential throughout the agency.

Several states have recognized that reports of suspicious transactions are a criminal intelligence resource. However, how this resource is used by these states is limited, in contrast to how federal authorities can use it, because the type of information available to each state differs.

To counter these investigatory problems, recent agreements and proposals made by the U.S. Department of the Treasury, the IRS, and others indicate that the difficulties associated with how suspicious transactions are reported are being addressed. If properly implemented, these steps could provide for the consistent and centralized management of suspicious financial transactions.

On the international scene, there have been a number of significant developments regarding money laundering. In late 1995, a presidential directive announced that U.S. agencies intend to identify and, if necessary, impose sanctions on the most egregious offenders among governments and banks that analysis indicates are facilitating the movement of proceeds of a variety of serious crimes, including drug trafficking, arms smuggling, sanctions violations, and other offenses.

Other agreements on standards and objectives were reached at the conclusion of the 1995 Summit of the Americas Ministerial Conference on Money Laundering, which established an action plan for the 34 governments of the Western Hemisphere and continued support of the Financial Action Task Force (FATF), including the conclusion of the first round of mutual evaluations of each of its member states.

Other areas addressed were the consideration of proposals to update FATF's universally accepted 40 recommendations to reflect new typologies and methodologies, the beginning of evaluations of members of the Caribbean FATF (CFATF), the further enhancement of the Asian outreach program, the creation of a common forum for major international bankers and government policymakers, and the convening of an international conference of financial intelligence units.

U.S. agencies have increased cooperation with foreign governments on major money-laundering cases, and several financial center governments (such as the Bahamas and Panama) have adopted broad, new anti-money-laundering policies and laws, while a number of governments are in the final stages of presenting or adopting new legislation.

On October 21, 1995, President Clinton signed U.S. Executive Order 12978, utilizing the sanctions authority of the International Emergency Economic Powers Act for the first time against 80 designated individuals and businesses found to be significant foreign narcotics traffickers, including those who assist in laundering trafficker proceeds via financial transactions. The order blocks assets in the United States and U.S. banks overseas of these traffickers, their front companies, and individuals acting on their behalf, and prohibits U.S. entities from commercial and financial dealings with them. The Treasury Department periodically publishes a list of target companies and individuals and directs U.S. companies and banks to block the targets' assets and prohibit trade with them.

But even as these initiatives are undertaken, the problems confronting policymakers and enforcement agencies become ever more complex and pervasive. The reason? *Cybercurrency*—the movement of money by electronic transfer technology. It becomes a question of speed, encryption technologies, and, most important, anonymity.

The electronic transfer of funds is certainly not new in the United States or, indeed, most of the developed world. Large-scale and wholesale payment transactions in the United States and other nations have been conducted electronically for some time. What is new today is the expansion of electronic money technology in financial transactions by consumers and smaller, nonfinancial organizations—organizations in which the consumers are the criminals and the financial transactions are nothing more than electronic crimes.

PART ONE

International Dimensions and Responses

The number of governments that ratified the 1988 United Nations (U.N.) Convention against Illicit Traffic in Narcotics and Other Psychotropic Substances (the Vienna Convention) increased in 1996. Many important financial centers have now adopted legislation to curb drug-related money laundering. However, too many priority financial centers have still not adopted needed legislation or ratified the convention. There is also a substantial question of whether the drug-trafficking-oriented money-laundering laws that many governments adopted in the earlier part of this decade are adequate, given recent developments in money-laundering practices and new technologies used in banking.

Organized crime groups are increasingly a factor in major money-laundering schemes—and the multiple sources of their proceeds compounds the difficulty of linking the monetary transaction to a unique predicate offense like drug trafficking. Moreover, criminal organizations have distinct patterns of operation that vary from one part of the globe to the next. Russian *mafiya* groups have enlarged their presence in the Western Hemisphere and are becoming as much a concern as the traditional Italian/Sicilian Mafia, Colombian cartels, Asian triads, and Japanese *yakuza*.

Meanwhile, an increasing number of drug traffickers do not directly manage the laundering or conversion of their proceeds, but rather rely predominantly on professional money brokers. Such brokers are increasingly crafting effective schemes to evade normal monitoring, detecting, and reporting devices.

To understand money laundering as it is practiced today on a global basis, one has to appreciate money as a commodity. Professional money launderers differ little in this respect from corporate money managers. A corporate money manager enters the money markets of various countries where the corporation will need national currencies during the next year and buys or sells currencies in a constant effort to improve the manager's average position at the time of payment. Similarly, money launderers use a bidding system to buy or sell drug proceeds, especially U.S. dollars. Just as a sound investment portfolio contains stocks, bonds, and other monetary instruments, the money brokers vary their holdings.

HOW MONEY IS LAUNDERED

Like institutional investors who put a percentage of their money into hedge funds, money brokers and the drug traffickers and other criminals who employ them collaborate to minimize risk. The Colombian Cali cartel, for example, minimizes risk by selling a substantial portion of the drug proceeds it earns from the sale of cocaine in the United States. Mexican traffickers in heroin, cocaine, and marijuana do the same, often selling to the same money brokers in behalf of Cali or for their own accounts. These brokers will convert proceeds for a fee, or they will buy the proceeds at a discount. Given the high profit margins of the drug trade, discounts of 7 to 10 percent or even higher, depending on risk, are common. At the end of the day, Cali and other trafficking groups may own or control 50 percent or less of the initial drug proceeds. The following hypothetical example illustrates the options available.

Assume that the Cali cartel is moving $100 million over the rather porous border from the United States to Mexico and operating on a 75 percent profit margin (earnings minus costs). Just $25 million must reach Colombia to replenish the operating budget. Cali wants to net $60 to $65 million from the bulk of the cash, or $85 to $90 million in total. Brokers have a bid or discount range of 10 to 15 percent. Cali agents will attempt to sell $25 million on the "gray" market—supported by Latin and even U.S. businessmen who want to convert pesos or other currencies into dollars—and go into the gray market to avoid exchange rates or taxes or, when profit margins are narrow on U.S. goods that can be sold in their countries, to realize higher profits. These currencies, especially pesos, can be readily returned to Colombia. The amounts over which Cali or Mexican traffickers retain actual control will be influenced by prevailing discount rates, investment opportunities, current risk dynamics, and gray market demand more than by the presence or absence of laws. At the same time, the need for fluidity and convertibility—influenced by the strength or weakness of the Mexican peso and the status of U.S. investor confidence, among other factors—will leverage the rate at which Mexican banks will do business with brokers.

Perhaps $25 million more will be "consigned" to allegedly licit importers who use various invoice schemes, at a discount, to legitimatize the return of dollars to their countries. The textile trade is a typical cover. For example, a South American clothing manufacturer working with Cali will obtain a permit to export $20 million worth of suits to New York. The manufacturer actually ships $6 million worth of suits to the Aruba Free Zone, where they are repackaged and sent back to Colombia and sold at a discount. Meanwhile, covered by an export license, the manufacturer's agent picks up $20 million in drug proceeds in New York and returns it to Colombia.

The bulk of the $100 million will be deposited in Mexican banks, after which a number of schemes can be used. Commonly, the money will be wire-transferred to accounts in the United States. The Mexican banks will then issue checks drawn on its U.S. accounts, payable to individuals or corporations. These checks can be batched for resale in Latin America or deposited into foreign bank accounts.

Enforcement officials believe that as much as $10 billion in Mexican bank drafts are laundered through such schemes each year in Panama alone. While some of the trade is in contraband goods, these checks, certificates of deposit, and other financial instruments have also been used to pay for legitimate shipments. Gold trade in the Aruba Free Zone amounts to more than $200 million a year. The Mexican banks will also issue their own dollar-denominated checks up to a level that they think will not cause inquiries.

Such brokers offer as much as $500 million to a bank or another broker at a point or two below the official exchange rate. The offer is probably not for a single transaction, but reflects the amount of money a broker has at his disposal. However, transactions are increasing in size. One recent transfer reportedly involved $78 million that went through a U.S. bank in a single transaction.

Why then don't U.S. reports and economic indicators reflect this volume of money transfer? The answer is fairly simple: these kinds of transactions are designed to fall outside the scope of U.S. Treasury and other reporting. For example, U.S. banking laws do not require reports on bank-to-bank transfers, let alone transfers from one branch to another of a bank.

Some of this flow shows up in physical movements of currency back to the United States. Flows from Latin America (especially Panama, Paraguay, and Mexico) to Federal Reserve Banks are in fact in excess of the levels that can be explained by traditional commerce. However, currency does not have to leave a placement site physically. Banks are at least one generation or more beyond the period in which physical money was moved to settle accounts. Dollar settlements are accomplished through reciprocal balances. For example, a Mexican bank can wire $50 million to a bank in New York, which gives the Mexican bank instant credit on the latter's New York account because the Mexican bank has simultaneously given the New York bank credit for $50 million at the latter's Mexican facility. Rather than moving physical cash to New York, the Mexican outlet is more likely to transfer physical cash south, as individual checks wend their way through various payment schemes. However, some cash does move back to the United States in bulk, carried by Mexican transfer agents who are not required to declare currency when crossing the U.S. border north.

The U.S. economy is one unintended beneficiary of the kinds of swaps and schemes carried out in Mexico. The gray market enables Latin businessmen to buy goods and services here and pay for it with dollars that originated in the U.S. drug market. In sum, the schemes are real and, in fact, are becoming more complex and are being played out on a wider world stage.

ARE THE LAWS BEING IMPLEMENTED?

In the years since the 1988 U.N. Convention was adopted, and particularly since FATF issued its 40 money-laundering recommendations in April 1990, dozens of governments worldwide have enacted various countermeasures, but these laws' pace of implementation and scope of application vary.

A review of results reported by key financial centers about the generation of suspicious transaction reports indicates that several such centers have reporting ratios that are disproportionately small, given the volume of financial activity and diversity of enterprises in their systems. Such minimal results could be an accurate reflection of a low level of suspicious activity, but these results may indicate a law that is drawn too narrowly or a banking system that is not giving full-faith compliance.

In addition, it is difficult to assess how much newer electronic banking practices render banks more or less vulnerable to money laundering. Few governments have control mechanisms that adequately identify and trace such transactions.

Apart from financial institutions in which officials are complicit in a money-laundering transaction, such institutions are made most vulnerable by the combination of correspondent banking relations and electronic transfers. In 1995, the twin problems of regulating wire transfers and tracing wire transfers in pursuit of an investigation were close to being contained because FATF had reached agreement with the dominant system (Society for Worldwide Interbank Financial Telecommunications, SWIFT) and its key members on including in each transfer message information critical to identifying those who transmit, receive, and, especially, benefit as owners of transactions. Record keeping may have improved; however, over the past year there does not seem to be any diminution in electronic transfers of illicit proceeds. Control efforts are being sorely challenged by the creation of new, independent wire transfer services, some of which service small clusters of banks.

CORRESPONDENT BANKING

Regulators, money-laundering investigators, and international policymaking bodies like FATF are facing profound challenges from a banking world that not only knows no geographic horizons and is open 24 hours a day, but is increasingly interconnected, as large multinational banks extend their reach through not only branch and subsidiary networks, but correspondent relationships that cross the globe.

The concern is not with the growth or dominance of the largest banks or the extension of their networks, but whether standards of prudent supervision are maintained at every juncture in this web of correspondent banking. The emergence of active financial service industries, in every jurisdiction, capable of becoming active players on the electronic highway of superbanking emphasizes ever more the need for the vetting of transactions at the bank of origin. Today, there is no confidence that the current know-your-customer policies are sufficient to actually cover most financial transactions at their origin.

The scope of international banking was made clear at the 1995 winter meeting of the International Bank Security Association (IBSA). The world's 12 major financial centers (except Japan) have one or more banks or financial institutions among IBSA's 52 voting members and six associate members, and these banks include many of the world's largest international banks.

An IBSA survey showed that 27 of these 58 banks have headquarters offices and/or branches in 146 countries. A separate survey showed that 19 of the 58 members own percentages (and sometimes controlling interest) in 144 other banking institutions. The actual "reach" of these big banks, both in terms of branches and holdings, is far greater; only 27 of the 58 responded to the surveys on branches.

While FATF has conducted an extensive external relations program, which has engaged an estimated 65 governments outside its own 26-member roster, no single agency, not even the

United Nations Drug Control Program (UNDCP), has accepted the responsibility for ensuring uniform standards of anti-money-laundering enforcement or bank regulation among all nations and territories.

OFFSHORE BANKING

Concerns about the regulation of offshore banking has not lessened over the past few years. The assurance of absolute secrecy by many jurisdictions that license such facilities makes it possible for such facilities to be manipulated to move and conceal or generate illicit proceeds. While the Offshore Group of Banking Supervisors (OGBS) continues to promote adherence to FATF countermeasures among its members, most offshore facilities have not been evaluated by FATF, OGBS, or other organizations, and far too many questions remain about the regulation of such facilities. FATF has completed evaluations by outside experts of its own members that have offshore facilities, such as Switzerland and Singapore.

The concern about regulating offshore facilities remains high with respect to most governments that issue such charters, but nowhere more so than in the Caribbean. The Bank of International Settlements has estimated that $5 billion of the $12 billion that is transacted annually through offshore facilities involves Caribbean offshore banks.

OTHER COMPLIANCE FACTORS

Other priority concerns that carried over through 1995 include the counterfeiting of currencies and other monetary instruments, especially bonds; the boom in contraband smuggling; the buying of banks and other financial institutions by suspected criminal groups; the resort by criminals to the use of smaller, less monitored banks; and the sophisticated use of such new phenomena as direct access and pass-through banking and electronic cash systems. There is continuing concern—given that financial crimes and money laundering occur with varying degrees of regularity in more than 125 jurisdictions—that some governments still have not criminalized all forms of money laundering. Some have not given sufficient regulatory authority to central banks and other institutions, many do not have adequate data systems to monitor trends and methods used in their territories, and many have not made adequate provision for mutual legal assistance.

CYBERCURRENCY

The use of microchip-based electronic money for financial transactions via smart cards and the Internet are assuming a potentially important place in the domestic and worldwide payments system. These chip-based cyberpayments are emerging very rapidly. Cyberpayments may soon become an addition to the major means of payment—currency, checks, credit cards, debit cards, and automated clearinghouse transfers—that are now used to make purchases.

Currency—paper notes and metal coins—has always been of particular importance in payments involving illicit activities. Currency attributes include ease of use, wide acceptability, and, most important from the standpoint of law enforcement, anonymity. The demand for the paper dollar is enormous. U.S. currency in circulation at the end of 1994 totaled approximately $405 billion. Of this amount, foreign holdings were approximately $270 billion. A significant feature of the new cyberpayments is that they include a new form of currency—a cybercurrency that is engineered to be an electronic emulation of paper currency. Cybercurrency includes the attributes of conventional currency: a store of value, a medium of exchange, a numeraire, anonymity, and ease of use.

But it has added features: transfer velocity (almost instant electronic transfers from point to point) and substitution of electrons for paper currency and other physical means of payment. Obviously, this is an innovative addition to the payments mechanism, but it requires close attention since the use of microchip and telecommunications technologies adds some significant new dimensions for law enforcement.

Yet cybercurrency is not the only monetary instrument innovation. Cyberpayments also comprise other payment components. Already in use or design are cyberchecks, an emulation of paper checks; cybercredit; cyberdebit; and so on. Furthermore, cyberpayments can replace or substitute for conventional wire transfer and financial message systems. In the next few years, cyberpayments will to some degree substitute for and supplement all current means of payment and a variety of monetary instruments.

This new technology raises many issues, including whether such payments constitute legal tender and are susceptible to monetary reporting and supervision measures. Must reporting regulations be completely redesigned to include the reporting of currency in electronic form moving to other countries via the Internet or across the border in a smart card or electronic purse? Law enforcement issues likely to arise in this area include fraud, counterfeiting, and computer hacking. Moreover, high-speed worldwide transfers that are a facet of the cyberpayment technology add complexity to law enforcement's ability to trace criminal activity and recover narcotics proceeds.

CONCERNS

More than 100 governments have ratified the 1988 U.N. Convention, including the great majority of high- to medium-priority governments. However, inconsistent enforcement of its anti-money-laundering provisions is an important factor in the continued high level of global financial crime.

Eight governments ranked as high, medium-high, or medium-priority money-laundering concerns by the U.S. government have signed but not ratified the 1988 U.N. Convention, and three other governments ranked among the higher priorities have not yet signed. Thus, almost one-fifth of the 67 governments in the three highest-priority categories have not ratified this universal accord 10 years after its declaration. (Part two of this book provides a country-by-country analysis of international laundering concerns.)

Too many affected or vulnerable governments have not criminalized all forms of money laundering and financial crime, nor given sufficient regulatory authority to central banks. There is a need for an intensified education and persuasion effort by the world's major financial institutions and organizations to ensure a higher level of compliance globally.

Too many governments continue to place limitations on money-laundering countermeasures, particularly the requirement that the offense of money laundering must be predicated upon conviction for a drug-trafficking offense.

Finally, too many governments still refuse to share information about financial transactions with other governments to facilitate multinational money-laundering investigations.

There is a critical need for enhanced bilateral and multilateral international communications to inform governments and financial systems in some systematic and ongoing way about the methods and typologies of drug- and non-drug-related money laundering and financial crime.

The layering and integration stages of money laundering are using more sophisticated money-laundering techniques. Cash is now being held in bulk or placed into the financial system through exchange houses and other nonbank financial institutions. Not only is it moved through wire transfers but innumerable varieties of licit and illicit financial instruments, including letters of credit, bonds and other securities, prime bank notes, and guarantees, without a parallel increase in the capability of the far-flung elements of the world's financial system to verify the beneficiaries or authenticity of instruments.

The electronic highway now links banks and nonbank financial institutions worldwide to facilitate expanding world trade and financial services, placing ever-greater priority on banks of origin to establish the identity of beneficial owners and their sources of funds. There are few controls on electronic transfers, and, compounding the problem, the bank or nonbank of origin is increasingly based outside major financial centers in jurisdictions that do not adequately control money laundering and other financial crimes.

Narcotics money launderers have adopted the invoicing schemes used by contraband smugglers and are similarly manipulating commercial trade practices to move and convert illegal proceeds. The vast proceeds generated by both types of crime magnify the need for control mechanisms to address non-drug-related financial crimes.

There is emerging concern about new banking practices, such as direct-access banking that permits customers to process transactions directly through their accounts by a computer operating off software provided by the bank. This system limits the bank's ability to monitor account activity, such as of joint accounts and pass-through banking schemes that have been a traditional method of layering. Owners who benefit from funds can now manipulate the identity of the ultimate recipient of the funds without review by bank officers. Pass-through banking by itself poses myriad problems for regulators, by creating the ability of depositors to unilaterally create accounts within accounts, or even to provide quasi-banking services to off-line customers in a kind of bank within a bank. These new bank services can limit the utility of systems in place to have both originator and recipient information travel with the electronic funds transfer.

There is continuing concern that the need for capital of many financial systems overwhelms prudent banking practices and safeguards, with respect to deposits, loans, and underwriting practices, and contributes to the increasing problem of takeovers of banks and nonbank financial institutions by criminal groups.

The concern about the concentration of economic power in

drug cartels and other criminal organizations, and its potential translation into political power, now embraces the Caribbean, Europe, the Middle East, and Asia, as well as the Americas.

Professional money-laundering specialists sell high-quality services, contacts, experience, and knowledge of money movements, supported by the latest electronic technology, to any trafficker or other criminal willing to pay their lucrative fees. This practice continues to make enforcement more difficult, especially through the commingling of licit and illicit funds from many sources and the worldwide dispersion of funds far from the predicate crime scene.

Nonbank financial systems are still unevenly regulated in most parts of the world, especially at the placement stage for cash. The United States, which is taking a leadership role in regulatory nonbank financial institutions, is still drafting the regulations that would subject them to federal regulation. Nonbank financial institutions include a wide variety of exchange houses, check-cashing services, insurers, mortgagors, brokers, importers, exporters and other trading companies, gold and precious metal dealers, casinos, express delivery services, and other money movers of varying degrees of sophistication and capability. Even less regulated are the underground banking systems, like the "chop" houses of the Orient and the Pakistani *hundi* and South Asian *hawala* systems.

Asset forfeiture laws have not kept pace with anti-money-laundering investigative authority, much less with traffickers' wide-ranging schemes. There is a conspicuous gap between the number of institutions and accounts identified by government investigations with money laundering and the authority of many governments to seize and forfeit drug and money-laundering proceeds.

Many banking systems remain obliged to inform account holders that the government is investigating them and may seize their accounts, providing criminals the opportunity to move assets and leave town.

Consequently, there is an urgent need to prescribe corporate as well as individual sanctions, including actions against financial institutions that repeatedly fail to take prudent measures to prevent their institutions from being used to launder money. Too, there is a need for continuous fine-tuning of bilateral and multilateral strategies that define responsibilities and objectives country by country and set specific goals for cooperating with the varying money-laundering and money-transit countries.

Many governments and financial systems continue to rely on voluntary reporting mechanisms, despite the inadequacy of voluntary control systems. Reports from government after government demonstrate that the adoption of mandatory controls has not caused declines in legitimate deposits or resulted in threats from traffickers.

Prudent supervision of many domestic banking systems has improved with respect to money laundering, but foreign branch offices, subsidiaries, and other foreign operations continue to figure prominently in drug and other money-laundering and financial crimes. There is a particular need for major international banks to ensure that governments and regulatory agencies in all jurisdictions they serve are enforcing the same high standards as charter governments. Yet, in reality, many governments seek to superimpose money-laundering controls on systems that still employ loose incorporation standards and permit bearer share ownership, which vitiate the impact of these controls.

The implementation of free-trade agreements and regional compacts, creating trading and economic zones that transcend national borders, could increase the use of international trade as a mechanism for laundering proceeds of criminal enterprises. The impact of the liberalization of border and other customs controls, liberalized banking procedures in these zones, and freedom of access in the zones creates additional potential risks for the future.

There is a need for countries that cooperate on money-laundering investigations and prosecutions to share forfeited proceeds so as to reflect equitably their respective contributions. A finders-keepers approach is unfair and fails to provide an incentive for multinational efforts.

SUGGESTED COUNTERMEASURES

In an electronic world in which the banking system operates through chain-linked computers 24 hours a day, there must be increased emphasis on thorough vetting of personal, company, and financial institution accounts at the bank of origin, wherever in the world it is located. There is no substitute for a thoroughly applied know-your-customer policy, especially as applied to those customers placing currency into the system and converting it to an account susceptible to immediate transfer outside the jurisdiction.

Considerable attention must be focused on establishing international standards, obtaining agreements to exchange information, establishing linkages for cooperative investigations, and overcoming political resistance in various key countries to ensure such cooperation.

Governments need laws that do the following:

- Establish corporate criminal liability for bank and nonbank financial institutions
- Apply to all manner of financial transactions not limited to cash at the teller's window
- Apply reporting and anti-money-laundering laws to a long list of predicate offenses not limited to drug trafficking
- Criminalize investments in legitimate industry if the proceeds are derived from illegal acts
- Enable the sharing of financial and corporate ownership information with law enforcement agencies and judicial authorities

But governments also need strategies (end games, if you will) that project change and progress along the same continuum as the changes in both financial system procedures and the methods criminals develop to exploit them—strategies that focus on specific governments and specific financial systems.

Over time, a number of actions can be seen as needed on a continuing basis to keep pace with the dynamics of money laundering in a high-tech world. They include, but are not necessarily limited to, the following 15 activities:

1. *Constant monitoring of money-laundering patterns, trends, and typologies.* More sophisticated techniques, involving both bank and nonbank financial institutions, in a wider array of traditional and nontraditional financial center countries have complicated identification, tracing, and investigation. Information exchanges have been improving, but critical gaps in know-how must be closed in tandem with improved cooperation.

2. *Analysis of money management practices.* We need improved information from more countries on what factors influence traffickers and their money managers to use particular systems in specific countries, to keep reserves in cash versus other monetary instruments, and to invest rather than park funds. Interviews of arrested drug money managers are producing detailed profiles of money management schemes. The best data so far apply to the cocaine trade, but we need to develop the same level of knowledge about heroin and marijuana syndicates.

3. *Analysis of non-drug-related money laundering and other financial crimes.* Traffickers seldom invent new methods or practices of handling and investing money. In general, they rely on techniques perfected by corporations and individuals to shelter proceeds from taxation or to avoid strict currency controls. Terrorists, arms dealers, and other criminals similarly rely on standard measures used to shelter funds from taxation by legitimate enterprises. We need to

identify the parallels between drug money laundering and financial crimes of every description and achieve an equal capability to investigate and prosecute such crimes. A number of governments are willing to impose new restrictions on drug-related financial crimes but hesitate to apply such strictures to other forms of financial crime.

4. *Equating economic power with political clout.* The increasing concentrations of wealth among criminal groups in a number of jurisdictions is a concern, not only because of possible impacts on investments, real estate values, legitimate commerce, and government integrity, but also because these organizations have the wealth to make large campaign contributions to candidates who, in turn, agree to assist the criminals. We need to assess the national security and political implications of these shifts and accumulations of wealth for all financial centers where such wealth is being concentrated. Illicit funds and corrupt officials represent a continuing threat to democracy in literally every region of the world.

5. *Eliminating systemic weaknesses.* We need banks to maintain the same kinds of records on clients that are also financial institutions as they do for other customers and to report suspicious transactions by such clients when the same financial institutions are named repeatedly in investigations. Some currently available but underutilized mechanisms include revocation of licenses, changes in ownership and management, collection of fines, and prosecution.

6. *Assessing the trafficker as entrepreneur.* We need to explore the extent to which criminal organizations are penetrating legitimate financial and other businesses and using the businesses' vast resources to gain control and to influence economic, financial, and business decisions. More data and systematic analysis are needed on the role played by the trafficker and money launderer in foreign-exchange markets, including their use of and creation of gray markets.

7. *Analyzing the impact of money laundering on national govern-ments and economies.* The interplay between political and structural factors in a country upon its receptivity to money laundering, and the effect of money laundering on the polit-ical life and economic life of the jurisdiction, needs to be better understood. Among the questions that need to be analyzed are the extent to which structural macroeconom-ic factors—such as commodity deflation, sustained high lev-els of unemployment, and recession—have in making a country susceptible to becoming a money-laundering haven. At the sector level, we need to determine the influ-ence of black markets on legitimate enterprises. At the insti-tutional level, we need to identify the major factors that may influence bankers and other financial managers in some jurisdictions to be more likely to accept money they have reason to believe is tainted. As we better identify where money laundering is most likely to have a macroeconomic or political impact, we need to evaluate the potential effec-tiveness of economic countermeasures. These could include limiting or excluding access to the global financial system of entities or states identified as major problems.

8. *Regulating exchange houses and remittance systems.* There is ample evidence that the various hundi, hawalla, and chop remittance systems, so essential to economic life in the Middle East and South and East Asia, are being used by drug traffickers, just like the *cambios* (exchange houses) of Latin America and nonbank institutions of all kinds in the Western financial community. They serve vital functions for key sec-tors of many economies. Systems for regulating them to dis-courage their use to launder the proceeds of crime are essen-tial but will fail unless these systems take into account the very informality that makes them effective and desirable.

9. *Concentrating efforts for maximum effectiveness.* Enforce-ment operations have proven that we can disrupt cartel operations. But these organizations are resilient and recov-

er quickly. We need to develop more effective strategies for disruption in order to achieve the destabilization of criminal organizations.

10. *Pursuing a continually evolving strategy.* For much of the 1980s, concerned governments operated under a strategy that involved a handful of key countries whose cooperation was essential or that were drug money-laundering centers. But the traffickers have changed tactics and moved to new locales. Banks are but one portal. They also use securities brokers, insurance companies, and import and export companies. Every means the worlds of business and finance have to offer, linked by wireless and facsimile transmissions, are today used by traffickers and the managers of their illicit proceeds. Financial regulation, supervision, and enforcement need to expand to cover both the transactions that transcend national boundaries and the widening array of types of financial service businesses.

11. *UNDCP should intensify its efforts to ensure that all significant financial center countries are implementing fully the anti-money-laundering and asset forfeiture provisions of the 1988 U.N. Convention.* As an immediate priority, the UNDCP should focus on securing ratification by the 12 significant financial center governments that have not yet ratified the convention.

12. *FATF, working with the OGBS and other relevant organizations, should focus increased attention on offshore banking.* FATF has been quite effective in reaching out to this group; a majority of offshore banking centers are either members of FATF or the CFATF, or, have participated in FATF/CFATF seminars that provided guidance on adopting or implementing FATF and U.N. guidance. More analysis is needed of the methods used to move money through offshore banks, and OGBS should be supported in its efforts to include as many offshore banking centers as possible in its membership and in its parallel effort to evaluate progress by its members.

13. *The adoption by governments of information standards recommended by FATF and the SWIFT banking information network is a welcome if not yet universal step.* Many more governments need to cooperate in adopting regulations to help curb the misuse of electronic transfer and payment mechanisms to launder illicit funds.

14. *Governments and banking systems alike must be more vigilant in efforts to detect counterfeit currency and other monetary instruments.* The schemes involving counterfeit bonds and other securities, usually as collateral, suggest that there is a need for an international clearinghouse to assist banking and financial systems outside the major centers in determining the authenticity of offered documents.

15. *Governments and banking systems must exert greater efforts to identify and prevent a wide range of financial crimes, not just drug and non-drug money laundering, but also financial frauds, such as prime bank guarantees.* Again, the history of such frauds suggests a need for a clearinghouse that can assist financial houses in identifying customers and authenticating documents.

U.S. PRESIDENTIAL INITIATIVES

In a speech to the United Nations in October 22, 1995, President Clinton announced a new U.S. initiative against money laundering. The president declared that those governments that were identified by the United States as being egregious centers for money laundering and that did not take corrective action could be subjected to sanctions. The initiative, which is known by its authorization as Presidential Decision Directive 42, includes within its scope not only drug-related but other types of money laundering, and also financial crimes associated with arms and contraband smuggling, nuclear proliferation, financing of terrorist groups, organized crime activities, and violations of U.N. or U.S. sanctions.

As a follow-up to the president's speech, the U.S. government has developed and is implementing the following two complementary analytical processes: (1) the categorization of each country's money-laundering vulnerabilities (based on generally accepted standards of judging anti-money-laundering laws, the adequacy and level of enforcement of these laws, and the degree of international cooperation); and (2) an assessment of the threat to U.S. national security that money laundering poses related to certain key criminal activities, including narcotics trafficking.

This process yields for the United States a list of priority countries to approach about specific shortcomings in their anti-money-laundering laws and enforcement efforts. The initial work with these countries will be based on diplomatic negotiation. President Clinton stated at the time of his U.N. speech that failure to change a nation's status as an egregious money-laundering haven could result in the imposition of sanctions, up to denial of access to the U.S. banking system.

TREATIES AND AGREEMENTS

Mutual legal assistance treaties (MLATs) are negotiated by the U.S. Department of State in cooperation with the Department of Justice to facilitate cooperation in criminal matters, including money laundering and asset forfeiture. They are in force with 19 governments, including Argentina, the Bahamas, Canada, Italy, Jamaica, Mexico, Morocco, the Netherlands, Panama, Spain, Switzerland, Thailand, Turkey, the United Kingdom with respect to its Caribbean dependent territories (the Cayman Islands, Anguilla, British Virgin Islands, the Turks and Caicos Islands, and Montserrat), and Uruguay. MLATs have been signed but not brought into force with eight other governments: Austria, Belgium, Colombia, Hungary, Korea, Nigeria, the Philippines, and the United Kingdom. Similar treaties are in various stages of negotiation elsewhere. The United States also has signed the Organization of American States (OAS) MLAT.

In addition, the United States has entered into executive agreements on forfeiture cooperation, including (1) an agreement with the United Kingdom providing for forfeiture assistance and asset sharing in narcotics cases, (2) a drug-related forfeiture agreement with Hong Kong, and (3) a forfeiture cooperation and asset-sharing agreement with the Netherlands (but not yet in effect with Aruba and the Netherlands Antilles). The United States has asset-sharing agreements with the Cayman Islands, Colombia, Ecuador, and Mexico.

Financial information exchange agreements (FIEAs) are bilateral executive agreements that facilitate the exchange of currency transaction information between governments. An FIEA provides a mechanism for exchanges of such information between the U.S. Treasury Department and another government's finance ministry. The ability to quickly exchange currency transaction information in money-laundering matters aids in achieving mutual enforcement goals. The United States has FIEAs in effect with Colombia, Ecuador, Panama, Paraguay, Peru, Mexico, and Venezuela. Each FIEA requires that both parties enact or have legislation that requires the reporting or recording of large currency transactions conducted at financial institutions.

On December 2, 1995, the Financial Crimes Enforcement Network (FinCEN) signed a memorandum of understanding (MOU) with the government of Argentina. The MOU was formulated within the framework established by the Summit of the Americas, December 1994, and its Ministerial Conference Concerning the Laundering of Proceeds and Instrumentalities of Crime, December 1995.

The parties agreed to provide each other with general information relating to money laundering, illicit drug trafficking, and related crimes, including information on trends and patterns involving the proceeds of drug trafficking or the international transfer of illicit assets. The parties also agreed to furnish one another with information about financial transactions, in coordination with appropriate authorities in each case, involving particular investigations of illicit activities or operations.

The seven FIEAs currently in effect differ in scope, providing for the exchange of information in three categories: (1) financial transactions associated with money laundering as a result of narcotics trafficking, (2) financial transactions associated with money laundering regardless of source of funds, or (3) financial transactions associated with illicit activities, not limited to money laundering.

Generally, requests for information and information provided must be case specific, tied to a violation of law, and requested in writing including as much identifying information as possible. Information provided must be used only for the purpose requested and not be further disseminated, disclosed, or transmitted without the written approval of the provider of the information. In urgent circumstances, the FIEA with Mexico allows for requests to be made by telephone or telefax, followed by a written request.

Although FIEAs are potentially a highly valuable tool for obtaining financial transaction information from foreign countries in support of money-laundering investigations, few requests have been made—with the exception of Mexico, which has actively used the FIEA to obtain financial transaction information from the United States in furtherance of its anti-money-laundering efforts.

U.S. Customs has mutual assistance agreements with Argentina, Australia, Austria, Belarus, Belgium, Canada, Cyprus, the former Czechoslovakia (now extended to the Czech Republic and Slovakia), Finland, France, Germany, Greece, Hungary, Italy, Korea, Mexico, Norway, Poland, Russia, Spain, Sweden, the United Kingdom, and Yugoslavia. Customs has negotiated agreements with other countries that are not yet in force, Denmark and Honduras being but two.

FINANCIAL INTELLIGENCE UNITS

FinCEN took the first concrete steps in an effort to establish an international network of the specialized anti-money-laundering organizations known as financial information units (FIUs). In June 1995, representatives of twenty-four nations and eight international organizations met at the Egmont-Arenberg Palace in Brussels to discuss FIUs.

Chaired jointly by FinCEN and the Cellule de Traitement des Informations Financières of Belgium, the meeting in Brussels enabled participants to become acquainted with the already existing FIUs and to open communication channels. It initiated discussion among these organizations on practical ways for sharing information. The issues identified by the Egmont Group continued to be developed through the efforts of three working groups and were once again addressed in a subsequent Egmont meeting in Paris in late 1995.

The Egmont Group is an unofficial organization of the several dozen FIUs in existence thus far. The existence of the group is a reflection on the success of FATF Recommendation 24: the creation of a centralized authority to take in and analyze suspicious transaction reporting.

FinCEN has launched an FIU orientation program for foreign counterpart agencies. This initiative contributed significantly to the enhancing of the cooperation between these agencies. Beginning with three representatives from the Netherlands Transaction Disclosure Office (Meldpunkt Ongebruikelijke Transacties, MOT), FinCEN provided a two-week structured series of briefings on its various functions and responsibilities. A one-week version of the orientation was repeated for a seven-member delegation of Polish officials responsible for drafting legislation that will establish an FIU in that country. In France, a two-week program was used for a representative from France's Traitement du Renseignement et Action Contre les Circuits Financiers Clandestins.

FinCEN became more involved in assisting countries of Eastern Europe and the former Soviet Union in establishing FIUs. Finding widespread support among Polish officials for the creation of such a unit, FinCEN organized a money-laundering seminar in Warsaw for approximately 40 government officials in February 1995. The conference also included participation by representatives from Belgian, British, and French FIUs. The Polish Ministry of Finance has taken the lead in sponsoring necessary legislation to create an FIU. In September 1995, FinCEN met with officials of the Russian government to discuss holding a similar seminar in Moscow. The Russian response was positive, but by no means conclusive.

In 1995, FinCEN began working with the Interpol Proceeds of Crime Group (FOPAC) on an analytical project to assess the money-laundering situation in countries of Eastern Europe and the former Soviet Union. FinCEN and FOPAC worked to develop a questionnaire for use during visits to each of the 23 countries encompassed by the project. The questionnaire addresses money-laundering trends, the financial services sector, and relevant legislation for use in information gathering. This is currently an ongoing process and, since its inception, FinCEN and FOPAC representatives continue to visit countries in the region, including Estonia, Latvia, Lithuania, Russia, Romania, Moldova, and Poland.

TRAINING AND TECHNICAL ASSISTANCE

The U.S. Department of State's Bureau for International Narcotics and Law Enforcement Affairs, Office of International Criminal Justice (INL/ICJ), coordinated multiagency Freedom Support Act (FSA) and Support for Eastern European Democracies (SEED) training. INL/ICJ, in cooperation with numerous other U.S. law enforcement, regulatory, and training agencies, offered international courses in Eastern Europe and the newly independent states (NIS) of the former Soviet

Union. The Bureau of Alcohol, Tobacco, and Firearms (BATF or ATF) participated in alcohol and tobacco taxation/licensing training in Russia and trained Russian, Latvian, Estonian, Polish, and Ukrainian students in post-blast investigations. The Federal Bureau of Investigation (FBI) provided white collar crime/financial crimes training in Russia. FBI provided instruction on organized crime and financial institution fraud in the Czech Republic, Estonia, Hungry, Latvia, Lithuania, Poland, Russia, Siberia, Slovakia, and Ukraine. Additional FSA and SEED courses taught by the FBI included DNA forensic training, international auto theft investigation, internal investigations, financial crime seminars, organized crime seminars, and instructor development.

FinCEN's international training program has two main components: (1) instruction provided to a vast array of government officials, financial regulators, and others on the subjects of money laundering and FinCEN's mission and operation, and (2) training on financial intelligence analysis and creation and operation of financial intelligence units, modeled after FinCEN.

FinCEN works closely with other agencies in supporting U.S. interests overseas. It participates in the Department of State Democracy and Law Program in Russia, the NIS, and Eastern Europe, as well as Ecuador and Panama. FinCEN's involvement encompasses (1) advising officials on how to establish advanced systems for detecting, preventing, and prosecuting financial crimes; (2) recommending ways in which to develop a partnership between government and financial institutions to prevent money laundering; (3) offering specialized training and technical advice in computer systems architecture and operation; and (4) providing assessments of money laundering risks as well as evaluations of anti-money-laundering laws, regulations, and procedures. While much of FinCEN's international training is done abroad, increasingly FinCEN is providing training to foreign senior officials at its headquarters in Vienna, Virginia.

Currently, FinCEN, under the auspices of the Egmont Group, is leading an effort to develop a curriculum on financial crimes and money-laundering intelligence analysis and on creating and running a financial information unit. The initial pilot course was offered in Europe during the summer of 1997, and training efforts will continue to expand internationally well into the 21st century.

SIGNIFICANT ENFORCEMENT CASES

Joaquín Guzmán-Lorea Drug Trafficking Organization: As a result of a three-year multiagency organized crime drug enforcement task force (OCDETF) investigation, a federal indictment was unsealed in San Diego on September 28, 1995, charging 22 members of the Guzmán-Lorea organization, including Joaquín Guzmán-Lorea (currently in custody in Mexico in connection with the killing of Cardinal Posadas Ocampo), with conspiracy to import more than eight tons of cocaine, as well as money laundering. The indictment also sought forfeiture of more than $700 million worth of money and property. This intensive OCDETF investigation involved cooperation among federal (DEA, IRS, Customs, and the INS) and local law enforcement agencies in San Diego, Los Angeles, San Antonio, Tucson, Newark, and Chicago.

Operation Green Ice, Phase II: On April 3, 1995, 18 indictments charging 80 U.S., Mexican, and Colombian defendants with money-laundering conspiracy and substantive counts were unsealed in San Diego, climaxing an international drug money-laundering investigation. The operation operated on three fronts: (1) to target check-cashing institutions (*casas de cambio*, exchange houses) operating along the U.S. Southwest border; (2) the creation of DEA "store fronts" purporting to launder drug proceeds, whose purpose was to identify drug money launderers and financial institutions receiving the proceeds; and (3) the use of the front to identify

31

Colombian money brokers. Arrests of 42 of the indicted individuals were made in Colombia, Canada, Los Angeles, Houston, Chicago, and New York. Seizures totaled in excess of $15 million, seven tons of cocaine, and sixteen pounds of heroin.

Operation Cornerstone: This two-year investigation culminated on June 2, 1995, with the unsealing of a nine-count indictment charging 59 individuals (including six criminal defense attorneys) with racketeering, drug trafficking, and money-laundering offenses. The investigation involved the U.S. Attorney's Office for the Southern District of Florida, the U.S. Customs Service, and the DEA. The investigation targeted narcotics trafficking and related illegal activities of the Rodriguez-Orejuela faction of the Cali cartel, which was responsible for at least 80 percent of the cocaine exported to the United States from Cali, and the indictment specifically charged the importation of more than 200,000 kilograms of cocaine into the United States.

District of Idaho: A plane was seized and forfeited in connection with the tracking of approximately $1 million laundered by the Steven Saccoccia international money-laundering organization, out of Providence, Rhode Island, and New York City, through various front-company bank accounts in Los Angeles, an aircraft broker's account in Denver, and ultimately to Boise. The plane was scheduled for delivery to Cali and was seized just days before the pilots were due to fly it out. The government sought forfeiture on the grounds that the plane was property involved in a money-laundering transaction and that it was being purchased by a Colombian broker for the Cali cartel to be used in the air shipment of cocaine. The aircraft was fitted in Boise with the latest in expensive avionics, including a global navigation system and other amenities useful for international trafficking. This case required substantial interagency cooperation, with assistance provided by agencies all over the country and successful sharing of information and resources.

Northern District of Illinois: A defendant's cooperation resulted in the forfeiture of more than $10 million in planes and drug money. The defendant, a Colombian national who operated a fleet of cargo aircraft that functioned as the "air wing" of the Colombian cartels and was used to smuggle at least 20 tons of cocaine into the United States, Canada, and Central America, was also sentenced to eight years in prison for narcotics importation conspiracy. The results of his cooperation also included the seizure of four Boeing 727s and a Convair 500 cargo plane in Colombia and the grounding of 26 other aircraft valued at $20 million at the Cali airport.

Eastern District of North Carolina: A forfeiture judgment was ordered against six defendants in the amount of $300,000 each after their convictions for conspiracy to distribute cocaine and marijuana and other related drug-trafficking offenses. The organization had successfully smuggled more than 50,000 pounds of marijuana and 500 kilograms of cocaine from Mexico through Arizona to the Eastern District. The investigation resulted in the arrest and conviction of a total of 23 defendants, with four fugitives at large. Additional results included the forfeiture of 17 pieces of real property valued at more than $4 million, the seizure or forfeiture of U.S. currency totaling $589,005, the seizure of four motor homes and 17 motor vehicles, the seizure of more than 2,100 pounds of Mexican marijuana and five kilograms of cocaine, and the issuance of two separate forfeiture judgments totaling $20 million and $1.8 million, respectively.

Western District of Washington: A shopping center and the drug proceeds of more than $4.5 million were ordered forfeit to the United States. The defendant in the case was also sentenced to life imprisonment and fined $4 million on his trafficking and money-laundering convictions. The defendant was the head of a criminal organization responsible for importing methamphetamine ("ice") from Korea and distributing it in the United States.

The defendant delivered more than 800 kilograms of ice to his distributors in the Seattle-Tacoma and Los Angeles areas, who then transported the ice to Hawaii, where it was sold.

Panama Money-Laundering Defendant Extradition: In the first money-laundering-predicated expulsion from Panama, on October 27, 1995, Israel Mordok, one of two fugitives from a nine-count 1992 indictment unsealed in 1994 in the Southern District of New York charging money-laundering (domestic and internationally exported currency structuring) violations, was arrested, stripped of his Panamanian resident status, and then immediately deported from Panama to the Southern District, where he pleaded guilty.

Certificates of Deposit: FinCEN responded to a federal agency request from Brownsville, Texas, concerning importations at Brownsville and Denver of $1 billion and $500 million in certificates of deposit issued by a Mexican financial institution. FinCEN research identified the Mexican company securing the CDs as a provider of short-term business credit. The courier was identified in DEA files as potentially involved in money-laundering activities and one of the U.S. companies was potentially identified as a subsidiary of a Connecticut holding company, originally incorporated in Delaware in August 1994. José Jesus Barrueta, a Mexican national, was indicted and pled guilty in March 1997 for laundering more than $17 million in drug money.

Argentina Request: FinCEN received a request seeking support in an investigation concerning subjects of an Argentine Federal Court of Criminal and Correctional Affairs investigation involving the Bank of Commercial Credit International liquidation process. Research and analysis revealed financial activity on three bank account numbers submitted with the Argentine request. Queries of the International Bank Security Association (BSA) database revealed case-related CMIRs (a report of international transaction of currency or monetary instruments, a U.S. Customs Service form) totaling $30,322 and currency transaction report (CTR, a U.S. Internal Revenue Service form) activity that totaled $409,250. Financial research also produced several previously unknown bank accounts, new leads, and elements common to the requester's investigation.

Russian Organized Crime: FinCEN provided support to a federal investigation involving Russian organized crime in the New York City area. Bank Secrecy Act transactions were discovered as well as property assets. In addition, FinCEN was able to organize and link the requester's subjects with associates and additional businesses. The case research provided enabled the investigator of this case to better understand and correlate his agency's intelligence.

Securities Fraud: FinCEN provided analytical support to a large securities fraud investigation at the state police level. This investigation was a multistate joint investigation looking into the activities of numerous employees and officers of investment firms. FinCEN discovered more than $2 million in currency transaction reports, more than $2 million in currency transaction reports by casinos, and approximately $7 million in property ownership records.

ASSET SHARING

Pursuant to the provisions of U.S. law, the Departments of Justice, State, and Treasury have aggressively sought to encourage foreign governments to cooperate in joint investigations of drug trafficking and money laundering, offering the inducement of sharing in forfeited assets. A parallel goal has been to encourage spending of these assets to improve narcotics law enforcement. The long-term goal has been to encourage governments to improve asset forfeiture laws and procedures and to undertake independent investigations.

From 1989 through 1995, the international asset-sharing program administered by the Department of Justice resulted in the forfeiture in the United States of $124,679,340.22 of which $42,209,368.29 was shared with foreign governments that cooperated in the investigations. In 1995, the Department of Justice transferred forfeited proceeds to the following countries:

Ecuador	$3,834,000
Switzerland	$2,098,000
United Kingdom	$523,393
Canada	$41,418
Israel	$34,770

Prior recipients of shared assets (1989-1994) include Argentina, the Bahamas, British Virgin Islands, Canada, Cayman Islands, Colombia, Costa Rica, Ecuador, Egypt, Guatemala, Guernsey (Channel Islands), Hungary, Liechtenstein, Paraguay, Romania, St. Maarten, Switzerland, United Kingdom, and Venezuela.

To date, Switzerland, Jersey (Channel Islands), and the United Kingdom are the only three jurisdictions that have shared forfeited assets with the United States as the result of the assistance of the United States to forfeitures effected under their own laws. In 1995, the United States also reached an asset-sharing agreement with Mexico that will serve as the basis to transfer forfeited assets from the United States to Mexico in the future, as well as a reciprocal sharing agreement with Canada.

REPRESENTATIVE FINANCIAL ACTION TASK FORCE (FATF) ACTIVITIES

The Financial Action Task Force (FATF) was established by the G-7 Economic Summit in Paris in 1989 to examine measures to combat money laundering worldwide. In April 1990, the FATF issued a report with 40 Recommendations that, when implemented, establish a framework of comprehensive programs to address money laundering and facilitate greater international cooperation.

FATF membership comprises 26 jurisdictions and two regional organizations, representing the world's major financial centers. Member jurisdictions are committed to adopting and implementing the 40 FATF Recommendations and agree to have their implementation progress evaluated by other FATF members.

In the mid-1990s, the FATF focused on several major areas in its fight against global money laundering. An experts group met to assess recent trends in money laundering, emerging threats, and effective countermeasures. Among the topics discussed was review of information available on money laundering in the securities and insurance industries. The FATF also completed the first set of mutual evaluations of its members' progress in implementing the 40 FATF Recommendations. In 1996, the second round of mutual evaluations began, focusing on the effectiveness of each member's anti-money laundering measures in practice.

The stocktaking review of the 40 Recommendations is a continuing process, with systematic measures being undertaken to ensure that the recommendations remain current and are updated as needed to effectively address today's money laundering situation. Emerging technologies, such as the cyber-currency phenemenon and its attendant vulnerabilities, are now central to the review process.

Through its external relations program, the FATF continues to encourage nonmember countries to adopt and implement the anti-money laundering measures outlined in the 40 Recommendations. During 1995, the FATF conducted high-level missions to Morocco, China, Korea, Macao, and Egypt to actively promote anti-money laundering action. During 1997, the FATF gave priority to its external relations efforts in Eastern Europe, the Caribbean, and Asia. Preliminary dialogues with Bulgaria, Russia, the Czech Republic, Indonesia, and the Philippines were initiated.

During 1995 and 1996, an experts group met in Hong Kong to assess money laundering methods specific to the Asia/Pacific region and counteractions indicated. In December 1995, the FATF and the Commonwealth Secretariat jointly conducted the

Third Asia Money Laundering Symposium in Tokyo, Japan. General agreement was reached to create an Asia/Pacific Steering Group on Money Laundering to provide a focus for anti-money laundering efforts in the region. The mandate for the Steering Group will be to encourage and facilitate the adoption and implementation within the Asia/Pacific region of the FATF 40 Recommendations, as well as to provide practical support to regional anti-money laundering initiatives including training and technical assistance. The FATF continues to coordinate extensively with other international organizations involved in combating money laundering and to mutually foster efforts in this area.

Five FATF members (United States, United Kingdom, France, the Netherlands, and Canada) continue to support and finance the Caribbean Financial Action Task Force (CFATF). The U.S. Treasury Department provided staff to the CFATF Secretariat, housed in Trinidad and Tobago. The CFATF continues to encourage its 26 member jurisdictions to implement the 40 FATF Recommendations plus 19 additional recommendations specific to the region. The CFATF has begun to conduct mutual evaluations of its members to assess their progress in implementing the 59 recommendations and a typologies exercise is being planned to assess current money laundering trends in the region.

Most recently, Italy chaired the eighth round of the Financial Action Task Force on Money Laundering (FATF). And during 1996-1997 several important tasks were conducted, in particular a broad-ranging review of money-laundering trends and techniques that included the specific examination of the threat posed by the development of new technologies in payment methods. The FATF also pursued its work in a number of areas concerning the implementation and refinement of anti-money laundering measures.

A major task conducted during 1996-1997 was the annual survey of money laundering methods and countermeasures that covered a global overview of trends and techniques. It was observed that the most noticeable trend is the increasing use by money launderers of nonbank financial institutions, in particular bureaux de change, remittance businesses, and non-financial rofessions. Special attention was paid to the money laundering threats of new payment technologies with the participation of private sector financial services experts. It was clear that law enforcement and regulators must look ahead now to identify potential problems and new challenges. Through continued partnership with the industry, the FATF intends to continue to study this issue as payment systems develop and to work toward the effective implementation of anti-money laundering measures before the system is abused. In the same spirit of cooperation with the financial services industry, the FATF addressed the issue of identifying the ordering client in electronic funds transfers and has examined ways to improve the provision of feedback to financial institutions.

A significant part of the FATF's work was dedicated to monitoring the implementation by its members of the 40 Recommendations. In addition, six mutual evaluations, focusing on the effectiveness of countermeasures in place, were conducted by Australia, the United Kingdom, Denmark, the United States, Austria, and Belgium. The FATF also completed two studies of measures taken by its members in the areas of confiscation of proceeds of crime and customer identification.

In cooperation with the interested international and regional bodies, the FATF pursued its task of encouraging nonmember countries to take action against money laundering. The round witnessed an increased involvement of the international organisations in discussions of FATF policy and external relations.

Also during 1996-1997, the FATF also reviewed its external relations strategy and working level relationships were increased with all the relevant organisations and in particular with the Caribbean Financial Action Task Force (CFATF). Application of the policy for encouraging other bodies to carry out mutual evaluations of their members' anti-money laundering measures commenced. In this respect, the mutual evaluation procedures of the CFATF, the Council of Europe, and the Offshore Group of Banking Supervisors (OGBS) were assessed as being in conformity with the FATF's principles.

The external relations activities of the FATF resulted in contacts and meetings with various countries of each continent. The formation of a regional anti-money laundering group in the Asia/Pacific region was very significant. At a Southern and Eastern African Money Laundering Conference, jointly sponsored by the FATF, the participants agreed in principle to establish a regional FATF. In Europe, FATF organized, together with the European Commission and the Council of Europe, a joint mission to Russia to advise on the need to implement a complete anti-money laundering system.

Finally, the FATF started to consider what will be the main challenges in the future for the international combat of money laundering. In this respect, the Task Force will undertake, in 1997-1998, an in-depth review of its future activities, structure, and membership. This task will be carried out under the Presidency of Belgium; it began on 1 July, 1997.

THE SUMMIT OF THE AMERICAS

At the 1995 Summit of the Americas in Miami, the heads of state of participating governments recognized that money laundering constitutes a serious challenge to the maintenance of law and order throughout the hemisphere and may threaten the integrity, reliability, and stability of governments, financial systems, and commerce. Action Item Six of the Summit's plan of action called for a working level conference on money laundering to plan a ministry-level conference that would study and agree on a response to money laundering by the Western Hemisphere.

The U.S. Departments of Treasury, State, and Justice worked with the other nations of the hemisphere to plan the

Summit of the Americas Ministerial Conference on Money Laundering, which was hosted by the government of Argentina, in Buenos Aires (November 30 to December 2, 1995). Following a six-country planning meeting on March 15, 1995, the first working-level conference was held on April 19–20, 1995, at Loy Henderson Auditorium, Department of State, Washington, D.C. All 34 nations were invited to send legal, financial, and law enforcement experts to attend this conference, and most countries were represented. The delegates began drafting a communiqué on money laundering that the ministers could issue at the conference. A second working-level conference was held at the same location in Washington on June 22–23, followed by a plenipotentiary conference at the Inter-American Development Bank in Washington, D.C., on November 20–21, where the communiqué was finalized.

The U.S. Departments of Treasury, State, and Justice coordinated the conference, which was chaired by U.S. Treasury Secretary Rubin and was attended by representatives of 29 of the 34 countries of the hemisphere. The conference also afforded an opportunity for bilateral talks on money laundering by senior U.S. officials. The conference demonstrated the commitment by governments in the hemisphere to a unified attack on money laundering. The communiqué set forth a set of standards and principles to promote transparency, oversight, and enforcement to stop money laundering. In further fulfillment of the summit's mandate, the ministers agreed to take all necessary measures, including legislative and administrative, in conformance with their nations' constitutions and laws to combat money laundering.

The communiqué established a Declaration of Principles in which the conferees agreed to make the laundering of proceeds a criminal offense. The ministers agreed on a plan of action that outlined legal, regulatory, and enforcement actions to be taken against criminal enterprises. Moreover, the participants agreed to institute an assessment of their progress in implementation of the plan of action in cooperation with the OAS. The conference also succeeded in creating an awareness that money laundering is a problem that goes beyond drug trafficking and involves other kinds of transnational crimes and that money laundering is not only a law enforcement issue, but also a financial and economic issue, requiring a coordinated interagency approach. When the principles and action strategies in the communiqué have been implemented and enforced by each government, there will be full compliance throughout the region with the 1988 U.N. Convention and the Organization of American States/Inter-American Drug Abuse Control Commission (OAS/CICAD) Model Regulations. In adopting the communiqué, the ministers made a commitment to do the following:

- Enact laws to criminalize the laundering of proceeds from serious crimes. The laws would provide for the identification, seizure, forfeiture, and equitable sharing between governments of such proceeds.
- Expand the tools available to police authorities in investigating money laundering and financial crimes, including the consideration of measures such as undercover police operations and judicially approved electronic surveillance.
- Review laws and regulations about bank secrecy and assess the extent to which these laws permit disclosure of financial institutions' records to competent authorities.
- Establish programs for reporting suspicious or unusual transactions.
- Share information among countries for the investigation and prosecution of money-laundering crimes and consider the direct exchange of financial information between countries.
- Create a center (FIU) to collect, analyze, and share with competent authorities all relevant information related to money laundering.

Discussion of the implementation of the communiqué was on the agenda of the 19th Regular Session of the OAS/CICAD meeting in March 1996. At that meeting, nations also agreed to submit to the OAS the establishment of a working group to consider an inter-American convention to combat money laundering. However, there seems to be little enthusiasm on the part of many members to actually addresss the issues. Consequently, aside from occasional public statements, real progress is minimal.

PART TWO

Money-Laundering Analysis by Country

Each year the United States has the task of ranking 201 nations and territories, using six categories that range from high priority to no priority. Rankings reflect a number of factors indicating that (1) this is the money-laundering situation in this nation or territory (i.e., drugs, contraband); (2) why the United States regards this situation as transcending local impact and having international ramifications; (3) the impact on U.S. interests; (4) whether the foreign government has taken appropriate legislative actions and the breadth of those laws; (5) whether the foreign laws are being effectively implemented; and (6) where U.S. interests are involved, the degree of cooperation between the foreign government and U.S. government agencies. Other factors are also considered and will be examined later.

It should be noted that a foreign government can have comprehensive laws on its books and conduct aggressive enforcement efforts, but still be rated as high priority if the volume of money laundering continues to be substantial and continued vigilance by this government is essential to the effectiveness of the overall international effort. When the severity of the money-laundering problem places a government in the top three categories and other deficiencies exist, the rankings will indicate that this government should take immediate action and will receive priority attention from the United States; conversely, as a government receives a lower ranking, remedial actions will have less immediacy or less impact for U.S. interests.

SELECTION CRITERIA

Since any financial system can be penetrated, every country and territory has the potential of becoming a money-laundering center. There is no precise measure of vulnerability for any financial system, but a checklist of what drug money managers reportedly look for provides a basic guide:

- Failure to criminalize the laundering of funds from all serious crime or limiting the offense to narrow predicates, such as conviction of a drug-trafficking offense, thus abetting efforts to commingle funds
- Rigid bank secrecy that cannot be penetrated by authorized law enforcement investigations
- Minimal or no identification requirements to conduct financial transactions, or widespread or protected use of anonymous, nominee, numbered, or trustee accounts
- No required disclosure of the owner benefiting from an account or the true beneficiary of a transaction
- Lack of effective monitoring of currency movements
- No mandatory requirement for reporting suspicious transactions, or a pattern of inconsistent reporting under a voluntary system, or a lack of uniform reporting requirements

- No recording of requirements for large cash transactions
- Use of monetary instruments payable to bearers
- Well-established nonbank financial systems, especially where regulation and monitoring are lax
- Patterns of evasion of exchange controls by nominally legitimate businesses
- Ease of incorporation, especially where ownership can be held through nominees or bearer shares or where off-the-shelf corporations can be acquired
- Limited or weak bank regulatory controls, especially in countries where the monetary or bank supervisory authority is understaffed, underskilled, or uncommitted
- Well-established offshore or tax-haven banking systems, especially countries where such banks and accounts can be readily established with minimal background investigations
- Extensive foreign banking operations, especially where there is significant wire transfer activity or limited audit authority over foreign-owned banks or institutions, or there are multiple branches of the foreign banks
- Limited asset seizure or confiscation capability
- Limited narcotics and money-laundering enforcement and investigative capabilities
- Countries with free-trade zones where there is little government presence or other oversight authority
- Patterns of official corruption or a laissez-faire attitude toward the business and banking communities
- Countries where the dollar is readily acceptable, especially countries where banks and other financial institutions allow dollar deposits
- Well-established access to international bullion-trading centers in New York, Istanbul, Zurich, Dubai, and Bombay
- Countries where there is a significant import in or export of gems, particularly diamonds

Again, this list is by no means inclusive, because not all countries will exhibit all patterns of activity, but it does provide an initial, albeit general, frame of reference when assessing the threat of a country's potential for housing money-laundering schemes.

ECONOMIC INDICATORS

The strength, vitality, and freedom of economies can serve as indicators of the relative vulnerability of a financial system to penetration by money launderers. Added to this are databases that introduce the element of relative black market activity, ranking virtually all sovereign governments on a scale of 1 to 5, with percentage of the gross national product as the defining factor.

Analysts assessing vulnerability can also use the existence of parallel economies as a measure (i.e., whether the parallel economy is seen as a major or minor factor in a given money-laundering situation).

Admittedly, there have been no empirical studies of this element, but confirmed information on money-laundering practices indicates that the parallel economy is a major factor in money laundering in a number of areas, including the following:

Burma
Colombia
Dominican Republic
Hong Kong
India
Mexico
Nigeria
Pakistan
Panama
Poland
Russia
Thailand

Venezuela
United States (the fungible economy that operates on both sides of the U.S.-Mexican border)

Parallel economies are considered a minor factor in the money-laundering situations in the following countries:

Argentina
Bolivia
Brazil
Chile
China
Costa Rica
Côte D'Ivoire
Cyprus
Ecuador
Greece
Guatemala
Hungary
Italy
Japan
Korea
Kuwait
Lebanon
Macao
Netherlands
Paraguay
St. Vincent and Grenadine
Taiwan
Turkey
United Kingdom
Uruguay

Parallel economies are not considered a significant money-laundering factor in the other governments in the high, medium-high, medium, and low-medium categories, and there are insufficient data to draw conclusions about the governments in the low and no-priority categories.

DEFINITION OF TERMS

In any analytical process, a clear understanding of basic nomenclature and its respective definitions is required. Analysis of the international money-laundering threat is certainly no different. Consequently, the following information is relayed to provide the reader with an introduction to fundamental terms:

- *Asset sharing.* By law, regulation, or bilateral agreement, a government permits sharing of seized assets with third-party governments that assisted in the conduct of the underlying investigation.
- *Compliance.* A government is meeting the goals of the 1988 U.N. Convention in terms of the effective application of implementing legislation.
- *Cooperation with domestic law enforcement.* By law or regulation, banks are required to cooperate with authorized law enforcement investigations into money laundering or the predicate offense, including production of bank records or otherwise lifting the veil of bank secrecy.
- *Cooperation with international law enforcement.* By law or regulation, banks are permitted or required to cooperate with authorized investigations involving or initiated by third-party governments, including sharing of records or other financial data.
- *Criminalized drug money laundering.* A government has enacted laws criminalizing the offense of money laundering related to drug trafficking.

- *Disclosure protection.* By law, a government provides a "safe harbor" defense to banks or other financial institutions and their employees who provide otherwise confidential banking data to authorities in pursuit of authorized investigations.
- *International transportation of currency.* By law or regulation a government, in cooperation with banks, controls or monitors the flow of currency and monetary instruments crossing its borders. Of critical weight here are the presence or absence of wire transfer regulations and the use of reports completed by each person transiting the country and reports of monetary instrument transmitters.
- *Maintenance of records over time.* By law or regulation, banks are required to keep records, especially of large or unusual transactions, for a specified period of time (e.g., five years). An effective know-your-customer policy is considered a prerequisite in this category.
- *Mutual legal assistance.* By law or through treaty, a government has agreed to provide and receive mutual legal assistance, including the sharing of records and data.
- *Nonbank financial institutions.* By law or regulation, a government requires nonbank financial institutions to meet the same customer identification standards and adhere to the same reporting requirements that it imposes on banks.
- *Non-drug money laundering.* A government has extended anti-money-laundering statutes and regulations to include non-drug-related money laundering.
- *Offshore banking.* By law or regulation, the government authorizes the licensing of offshore banking facilities.
- *1988 U.N. Convention.* A government has formally ratified the 1988 United Nations Convention against Illicit Trafficking in Narcotic and Psychotropic Substances.
- *Recording of large transactions.* By law or regulation, banks are required to maintain records of large transactions in currency or other monetary instruments. An effective know-your-customer policy is considered a prerequisite in this category.

51

- *Reporting of suspicious transactions.* By law or regulation, banks are required (or permitted) to record and report suspicious or unusual transactions to designated authorities. An effective know-your-customer policy is considered a prerequisite in this category.
- *System of identifying and forfeiting assets.* A government has enacted laws authorizing the tracing, freezing, seizing, and forfeiting of assets identified as relating to or being generated by money-laundering activities.

COUNTRY-BY-COUNTRY STUDY

Against this backdrop, a country-by-country analysis of the international money laundering threat, beginning with the priority ranking assigned to each country, can now begin.

Afghanistan
(Low.) Since little remains of Afghanistan's banking and commercial structure, its war-torn economy does not have the capacity to accommodate sophisticated money-laundering schemes.

Albania
(No priority.) This nation's proximity to major European drug markets; connections with organized crime in Italy, Turkey, the former Yugoslavia, and elsewhere; and the emergence of an active network engaged in migrant and arms smuggling across the Adriatic enable narcotics traffickers to stay well ahead of enforcement efforts. The beginnings of money laundering in Albania have been reported despite the poorly developed banking system. Incomplete criminal legislation and a corrupt and inexperienced judiciary hamper effective prosecution of criminal elements.

Andorra
(Low.) Although not a major financial center or money-laundering haven, Andorra has enacted strong laws. Any act designed

to conceal the origin of money or other assets derived from drug trafficking, prostitution, or terrorism by a person who is aware or should have been aware of that origin and any subsequent lawful use of such money or assets by that person are punishable by imprisonment and fines. Government law enforcement officials are investigating the possible use of the Andorran financial system by Colombian traffickers and money launderers.

Anguilla

(Low.) Money laundering is considered minimal in Anguilla, a dependency of the United Kingdom. In 1993, the United Kingdom and Anguilla allowed the United States to set up a "paper bank" in an undercover money-laundering sting operation that culminated in December 1994. This operation resulted in the arrest of 116 defendants and the seizure of more than U.S.$90 million in drug-trafficking assets.

Argentina

(Medium-high.) Argentina is an important regional financial center. Although a growing volume of money laundering is taking place in Argentina, the country is not yet considered a major money-laundering center. Some money laundering is related to narcotics proceeds, but much of it consists of illicit funds from tax evasion, bribery, contraband, and other illegal activities. A very large share of transactions in Argentine financial institutions are denominated in U.S. dollars and take place in cash.

In December 1995, the Argentine government hosted the Summit of the Americas Ministerial Conference on Money Laundering. Twenty-six country delegations participated. At this meeting, Argentine officials announced the government's intention to establish a financial crimes enforcement network like the U.S. Treasury's FinCEN. They also stated their intent to issue regulations that would require Argentine financial institutions to report large transactions, particularly those in cash.

There is no written agreement between the governments of Argentina and the United States about money laundering specifically, but the MLAT covers exchange of information and evidence. Argentina has numerous bilateral antinarcotics agreements with other countries, including cooperation against money laundering.

Money laundering is a criminal offense when explicitly linked to narcotics activity. There is no separate money-laundering law. There are no requirements for banks to "know, record, and report on" customers involved in suspicious transactions. There are no "banker negligence laws." Voluntary guidelines of the two banking associations of private banks suggest that banking records be kept for five years, but there are no legal requirements. Bankers are required by law to protect the identity of depositors, unless presented with a court order seeking specific information. The banking secrecy laws (incorporated in the central bank's charter) have left unclear how far bankers may go in voluntarily providing information in the absence of a court order. There are no controls on the import and export of cash or other financial instruments.

There have been few cases prosecuted that were related exclusively to money laundering. To date no successful prosecutions have taken place for money-laundering offenses. At the end of 1995, a federal judge ordered police to search 10 casinos in the northern provinces based on the suspicion that the casinos were being used as fronts for money-laundering operations. That investigation is still current.

Judicial and police officials systematically track assets when a narcotics arrest is made and seize assets when they are clearly connected with a narcotics crime. But narcotics traffickers can easily shield assets in Argentina. Although assets are seized by the police with court authorization, the police (who are responsible for tracking money laundering) do not have adequate powers or resources to trace and seize assets. The total amount of assets seized in 1995 is not known. Argentina reacts positively to U.S. efforts on this front and attempts to emulate U.S. success, including sharing of information among agencies. Argentina is active in the OAS on asset seizure discussions. National laws permitting sharing with other countries have not been tested, but the banking community cooperates informally in a limited way with law enforcement authorities on asset seizure.

Armenia

(No priority.) As a result of the economic recession and major deficiencies in the present banking system, the amount of money laundered in Armenia is insignificant.

Aruba and Netherlands Antilles

(High.) In 1996, the Netherlands Antilles joined Aruba on the high-priority list, reflecting increased U.S. concerns about the role that these two parts of the Kingdom of the Netherlands play in money laundering in this hemisphere. Offshore banking facilities, casino-resort complexes, the high volume of tourists, and stable currencies continue to make Aruba and the Netherlands Antilles attractive to money-laundering organizations. The government of neither entity has taken all the steps necessary to comply with international standards for money-laundering countermeasures, including ratification of the 1988 U.N. Convention.

In both Aruba and the Netherlands Antilles, money laundering has been a criminal offense since December 1993. The law contains many strong features, including a wide range of predicate offenses, a knowledge provision that allows for the prosecution of "willful blindness," a measure for corporate liability, and the provision of substantial penalties. Legislation establishing the legal requirement concerning customer identification and the reporting of unusual transactions became effective in both jurisdictions on February 1, 1996. The legislation also mandated the creation of a reporting center to analyze the reports of unusual transactions and, if necessary, to forward the reports to law enforcement for further investigation. The reporting centers became operational on February 1, 1996. These laws are supplemented and reinforced by the new *Money Laundering Guidance Notes* for banks and financial institutions issued by both central banks. The guidance notes set out detailed procedures concerning matters such as know-your-customer policies, sales of monetary instruments, bookkeeping and wire transfer operations, reporting requirements, internal banking policies and procedures, record retention, staff training, and the information to be provided to the central bank for its monitoring of money-laundering deterrence and detection procedures.

Aruba and Netherlands Antilles laws provide for the seizure and confiscation of proceeds or other property involved in or derived from money laundering or an underlying crime. A criminal conviction is a prerequisite for confiscation action, and it is necessary to prove that the money was directly derived from a specific crime. Proposed amendments to Aruba and Netherlands Antilles law will give authorities more flexible powers, including civil confiscation proceedings and seizure before a criminal prosecution has been initiated.

Monetary laws have been established requiring financial institutions to verify the origin of cash deposits of 10,000 florins or more in onshore banks in both the Antilles and Aruba, but this legislation does not apply to offshore facilities.

The pace of change has been disappointing, given the commitments both governments made to adopting FATF standards at a conference in Aruba in 1990 and their considerable participation in CFATF. There is a question of political will, since corruption is believed to be a factor inhibiting effective enforcement. The impact of the recently passed anti-money-laundering measures in both jurisdictions will depend on whether the laws being put into place are systematically enforced and cases of money laundering prosecuted.

Australia

(Low-medium.) Australia has pioneered money-laundering and cash-transaction reporting legislation designed to counter money laundering by organized crime. It is among the few nations that, like the United States, require direct reporting of significant as well as unusual transactions, and was the first to systematize the monitoring of wire transfers. The government ratified the U.N. Convention, participates in the U.N. Drug Control Program, and is a leading member of FATF. The Customs Act of 1901 and the Proceeds of Crime Act of 1987 allows for asset forfeiture and seizures in narcotics cases. The legislation is based on convictions.

Austria

(Medium-high.) Notwithstanding important improvements in its anti-money-laundering policies, the priority for Austria has recently been raised to medium-high, both because of continued shortcomings in overall policy and because of indications that Russian organized crime groups are using Austrian accounts to launder the proceeds of crime.

In 1994 new legislation took effect that requires all banks to report transactions suspected of involving money laundering. Government officials released the results of the first full year under the legislation (1994) in 1995: 346 transactions were reported as suspicious to the special force for organized crime, with accounts totaling 298 million Austrian schillings (AS) or U.S.$29 million at current exchange rates, blocked immediately by court order. In the first five months of 1995, Austrian banks reported 110 transactions, of which AS 386 million (U.S.$38 million) were blocked.

Although the regulation on suspicious transactions has proved useful, shortcomings still exist. Officials believe that the existence of anonymous securities accounts is a more significant problem. The government has submitted to parliament a penal code amendment to expedite extradition, expand judicial assistance, and enable courts to confiscate property and assets on the presumption that these stem from illegal activities, unless the accused can establish the lawful acquisition of the assets.

Anonymous passbook savings accounts are another problem area, representing 95 percent of the total of 26 million Austrian savings accounts in which U.S.$150 billion are on deposit. Only Austrian residents are supposed to be able to hold anonymous passbook savings accounts, but banks require no proof of residency when opening an account. Banks are required to know and record the identity of customers, but they are not required to report customers engaging in significant, large currency transactions unless they are suspicious. Banks and financial institutions must keep identification records until at least five years after termination of the business relation with the customer and vouchers and records of transactions until at least five years after their execution. On February 13, 1996, the European Commission formally demanded that Austria take steps to abolish anonymity for all bank accounts, stating that this facilitates money laundering and is inconsistent with European Union (EU) anti-money-laundering guidelines.

The Bahamas

(Medium.) The passage of the new money-laundering legislation reflects an increased emphasis by the Bahamas on combating money laundering. In addition to the new legislation, the current U.S.-Bahamas MLAT authorizes, as an exception to bank secrecy laws, access to records in cases of suspected narcotics money laundering. The Bahamas has agreed to an independent evaluation of its money-laundering controls by CFATF. The government requested, however, that the evaluation be postponed so that it would occur after the passage of the new money-laundering law.

The Bahamas has simplified procedures for registering shell corporations, known as international business companies (IBCs), which can issue bearer shares. Reporting requirements for IBCs, currently numbering over 38,000, are minimal, and they could be used by criminals to facilitate money laundering. Under Bahamian law, the assets of a convicted drug offender are subject to forfeiture. A procedure also exists for the civil forfeiture of assets that are the proceeds of trafficking or are used for trafficking. Over the past few years, the government has had difficulty making effective use of the asset forfeiture tools available to it, in part because of the delays that plague the country's legal system. During 1995, however, a joint effort by the Ministry of Finance and the attorney general's office seemed to be producing positive results in this area. Moreover, during 1995, drawn-out forfeiture proceedings against valuable real estate formerly owned by Carlos Lehder, a Colombian kingpin now jailed in the United States, were completed, with the Bahamas receiving uncontested title.

Bangladesh

(No priority.) There is no evidence of money laundering in Bangladesh. The Department of Narcotics Control proposed in 1994 to amend the 1990 Narcotics Control Act to encompass money laundering, extradition, and controlled delivery, but department officials say there has been no movement on this proposal. Provisions for court-ordered examination of financial records or confiscation of assets have been largely ineffective because of detailed burden-of-proof requirements that discourage poorly trained law enforcement officials from pursuing that avenue during investigations.

Belize

(Medium.) Money laundering is considered a major potential threat in Belize. More than 1,000 companies are registered under the International Business Companies Act. Belize Bank, a subsidiary of Belize Holdings, is the only entity authorized to register companies under the act. There are no laws in Belize making money laundering a crime. There are no laws regulating the movement of currency in Belize. Belize law also allows unrestricted use of bearer negotiable instruments to conduct financial transactions. Inadequate regulations governing offshore investments are of concern. In late 1996 the government of Belize passed new legislation governing this sector and is preparing legislation that will open up and govern offshore banking as well. Belize participates actively in hemisphere meetings that give rise to anti-money-laundering communiqués.

Belgium

(Medium.) Belgium is principally a transit country for illicit drugs bound for larger markets in Western Europe, but the recent volume of suspicious transaction reports suggests that Belgium is also a money-laundering center. Belgian law enforcement agencies see a continued increase in drug trafficking from Asia and the Middle East via the countries that formerly made up the Soviet Union. The report by the financial analysis unit to the Ministries of Finance and Justice on suspicious financial transactions showed 352 transactions in the first 10 months of 1995; the transactions were referred to prosecutors for further investigation.

A special unit set up in 1993 to look into suspicious transactions reported by banks and other financial institutions actually reports cases; from January 12, 1993, to June 30, 1995, the unit transmitted 211 cases, which involved 2,126 transaction reports. The large volume of cases and reports and the value of these transactions—more than U.S.$1 billion in the first 10 months of 1995—represent a significant volume for a country of nine million inhabitants.

A Belgian law of 1990 provides criminal penalties for officials of financial institutions who engage in money laundering under a "due diligence" test whereby it need only be established that the officials knew or should have known that the transactions involved proceeds from criminal activity. Reporting a suspect transaction effectively immunizes a financial institution from criminal prosecution, so coverage is believed to be effective. A shortcoming of the Belgian law is that the Ministry of Finance may only report to prosecutors cases in which there is evidence linking those involved in the transaction to specified criminal activities (including drug trafficking), rather than a blanket provision covering all serious crimes. Officials investigating these cases say that the majority involved exchange houses in Antwerp and Brussels used by non-Belgian residents to convert money from the currency of the country of origin (especially pounds sterling) into the currency of the ultimate destination (most commonly the Netherlands). Most of the rest of the total seems to be tax fraud transactions, mainly involving the value added tax.

The 1990 money-laundering law includes provisions to seize assets derived from illegal activities when sufficient specific, concrete evidence linking identifiable individuals is available to present to a court of law. However, asset forfeiture and seizure has been minimal to date. Belgium is a member of FATF and has implemented the EU Directive on Money Laundering. Belgium has ratified the 1988 U.N. Convention.

Benin

(No priority.) Benin is not considered an important financial center in West Africa or in the world. There is no effective policy to deal with money laundering in Benin. The laws on the books do not adequately address the issue. There are no requirements to report significant cash deposits in banks. Even if there were such requirements, it is questionable how effective they would be given Benin's large informal sector, which is essentially a cash economy. Significant cash deposits by market women are common and unremarkable. There are no indicators available describing the extent to which money laundering occurs in Benin, but determined money launderers in Benin probably do not have difficult obstacles to overcome.

Bolivia

(Medium.) With total bank deposits of little more than U.S.$2 billion, the Bolivian financial system is not a significant participant in international, or even regional, money laundering. Money laundering is not a crime under Bolivian law, which provides instead strict bank secrecy standards. To gain access to bank records, law enforcement authorities must first obtain a court order and then file a request with the superintendent of banks. International cooperation on record sharing is nil.

The Association of Banks has promulgated a code of conduct that calls on banks to be alert to the possibility of money laundering and to avoid dealings of a suspicious nature, but in the absence of sanctions and a relaxing of bank secrecy provisions, the code is likely to accomplish little. Resistance to change in the Bolivian financial sector reflects a long tradition of corruption, tax evasion, and contraband.

On the brighter side, Bolivia signed a new extradition treaty with the United States in 1995 that will explicitly include drug money laundering as an offense and require extradition of Bolivian nationals.

According to the prevailing interpretation of Bolivia's constitution, a seized asset belonging to a narcotics trafficker may only be forfeit after the trafficker is convicted. Because all cases must be appealed to the Bolivian Supreme Court, which is hopelessly backlogged, that can take years. While the case is in progress, maintenance and upkeep of seized assets is the responsibility of the government. On paper, the government has custody of more than $300 million in seized assets, but in reality it holds much less—the result of fraud, theft, and deterioration of properties. As a partial remedy, the government issued a decree in late December permitting the auction of seized assets with the consent of the owner, the proceeds becoming available to the owner if and when he is found innocent. This should prove attractive to the government and traffickers alike in cases where assets depreciate quickly or require constant care (e.g., new automobiles, cattle herds). The Bolivian government, with technical assistance from the U.S. Embassy, is developing mechanisms for using the revenues generated for counternarcotics purposes.

Botswana

(No priority.)

Brazil

(Medium-high.) Gauging money-laundering levels in Brazil is somewhat difficult, because of Brazil's failure to criminalize money laundering. A strong economy has increased the risk of money laundering in Brazil, and estimates of illegal funds circulating range from tens of millions to hundreds of billions of dollars. The Brazilian justice minister has stated that Brazil will become a haven for illegal capital if its controls continue to lag behind those of the rest of the world. There are reports of foreign criminal interests buying up such failing businesses as hotels, air taxi services, and transport, construction, and insurance companies to serve as repositories for the laundering of illicit profits.

On the international front, Brazil's lack of domestic legislation has limited its ability to cooperate with other countries in money-laundering investigations. The Brazilian government did contribute positively to a Buenos Aires money-laundering conference, and a U.S.-Brazil counterdrug cooperation agreement calls for the parties to adopt and implement appropriate legislation on money laundering and asset forfeiture. During 1995, two U.S. agencies (the Customs Service and FinCEN) presented seminars to Brazilian officials on measures to control money laundering, and the Brazilian president intends to submit legislation to congress criminalizing money laundering and establishing a financial crimes intelligence center. The law is expected to follow OAS/CICAD recommendations in terms of easing bank secrecy, requiring suspicious transaction reporting, establishing effective currency reporting systems, and setting adequate sanctions for noncompliance.

British Virgin Islands

(Low.) While sharing some of the vulnerability of other offshore centers, especially as a result of its chartering of international bearer share companies. Money-laundering activity in the British Virgin Islands is currently considered minimal by U.S. agencies.

Bulgaria

(Medium.) Bulgaria is not considered an important financial center, tax haven, or banking center in the region. Bulgarian officials consider Bulgaria highly vulnerable to money laundering in both the banking and nonbanking financial systems, although there are no hard data on its extent. The money laundering that does occur may relate to the sometimes illegal conversion of state assets to private hands and other forms of illegal trade, as well as to narcotics proceeds. There is no evidence that government policy or senior officials encourage, facilitate, or engage in money-laundering activities.

Bulgarian and U.S. law enforcement agencies generally cooperate well in counternarcotics investigatory efforts and information sharing. Information about in-progress Bulgarian criminal investigations subsequent to arrest is held in secret, but can be released to foreign law enforcement agencies at the discretion of the prosecutor's office.

Although Bulgaria has signed and ratified the 1988 U.N. Convention and is also signatory to the 1990 Council of Europe convention on laundering, search, seizure, and confiscation of proceeds from crime, it has not yet passed legislation on money laundering. Bulgaria has no bilateral agreements with other countries on money laundering, and although it does have under consideration a draft money-laundering law to reflect its obligations under the 1990 Council of Europe convention, money laundering is not now a criminal offense in Bulgaria, except in some cases where it constitutes criminal concealment of another crime. There have been no arrests or prosecutions in Bulgaria for money laundering, and the current lack of comprehensive financial legislation provides broad opportunities for traffickers to shield assets and launder money.

Banks are not currently required to report the identity of customers engaging in significant or suspiciously large currency transactions; the draft law under consideration would require banks to report large transactions only if they appear suspicious and would not require regular reporting. Although there is bank secrecy protection under the law, banks are required to keep records to reconstruct significant transactions through financial institutions to respond to information requests from the government on criminal matters. This requirement also appears in the draft law. Such money-laundering controls would be applied to money exchangers as well as banks.

There are controls on the ways money may be transferred into and out of the country. There are not, however, due-diligence or banker-neglect laws that make individual bankers responsible if their institutions launder money. The draft law would criminalize intent but not neglect in this regard.

Narcotics-related assets may be temporarily seized if directly related to a narcotics-related crime, but they cannot be forfeited except in the context of a judicial sentence. The public prosecutor can request seizure of a legitimate business if it is used to launder criminal proceeds and hence conceal criminal activity. Bulgaria enforces asset seizure or forfeiture if mandated in a judicial conviction or in a court decision under the commercial code.

Burma

(Medium.) The 1993 Narcotic Drugs and Psychotropic Substances Law brought the Burmese legal code into technical conformity with the 1988 U.N. Convention. As such, the 1993 law contains useful legal tools for addressing money laundering, the seizure of drug-related assets, and the prosecution of drug conspiracy cases. However, to date, these provisions remain largely unused because Burmese police and judicial officials have been slow to implement the law, targeting few if any major traffickers and their drug-related assets. The lack of vigorous enforcement against money laundering leaves Burma vulnerable to the growing influence of traffickers through the use of drug proceeds in legitimate business ventures.

Cambodia

(Low-medium.) Cambodia shares borders with Thailand, Laos, and Vietnam—the Golden Triangle of Southeast Asian heroin production and trafficking—a factor that, with indications of an emergent involvement in the movement of narcotics proceeds, recently raised its priority from low to low-medium.

Cambodia's five-year-old democracy, installed after elections in 1993, still faces an active, although diminishing, Khmer Rouge insurgency. Laws and legal institutions are still being developed. Enforcement agencies are also in the initial stages of operation. National and municipal police charged with antinarcotics (and indeed all) law enforcement activities lack training in basic law enforcement techniques and drug enforcement measures, including drug identification. They have no communications equipment and few facilities.

Cambodia has approximately 33 banks, but the national bank only recently received legal authority to regulate them. Previous attempts by the central bank to audit local banks are reported simply to have been thwarted by private guards hired by those banks. The Royal Cambodian Government, trying to deal with the effects of more than 20 years of warfare and internal strife, is heavily dependent on external assistance, and most ministries, including those charged with police functions, have only enough funds to cover salaries. The lack of funds for training and operations, coupled with the newness of the nation's democratic institutions, makes Cambodia a vulnerable target for drug traffickers and money launderers operating in Southeast Asia.

There are no empirical data about the current extent of drug trafficking and money laundering in Cambodia, but the size of one heroin seizure, coupled with anecdotal evidence, indicates a growing problem.

Cambodia's constitutional monarch signed a decree establishing a national counternarcotics authority, whose chairmen are Cambodia's two prime ministers and whose vice-chairman is the minister of justice. The ministry of justice, with the assistance of an adviser from UNDCP, concluded a draft of antinarcotics legislation that was recently reviewed by the council of ministers and is expected to be sent shortly to the national assembly. The legislation contains a provision outlawing the laundering of drug proceeds. The legislation commits the government to becoming a party to the 1961 Single Convention on Narcotic Drugs, the 1971 Convention on Psychotropic Substances, and the 1988 U.N. Convention.

Canada

(High.) Canadian officials estimate that 80 percent of money laundering in Canada is international (i.e., money laundering occurs either from profits generated from drug sales in Canada, which must be laundered and returned to the source countries, or from drug money generated abroad, particularly in the United States). Canada's advanced financial sector, lack of mandatory reporting requirements, and proximity to the United States make the country attractive to drug money launderers, especially for the placement of currency generated from the sale of drugs. Canada does not impose cross-border currency reporting. Its bankers continue to oppose mandatory reporting of suspicious transactions, while complying with other international standards for bank recordkeeping. Canada reports a high level of compliance with the voluntary reports.

According to a report issued by the Canadian Solicitor General, drug money laundering in Canada takes place in banks and deposit-taking institutions, currency exchange houses, front companies, real estate transactions, and gold shops. Banks are the most commonly used means to launder and move drug money because of the prominence of their branches in traditional tax haven countries, such as the Bahamas and other Caribbean nations. Currency exchange houses, particularly those located in cities along the U.S. border, are suspected of moving large amounts of drug money between the two countries. Currency exchanges, like banks and other financial institutions, are not required to report large or suspicious transactions to authorities, although they are required to maintain records of large cash transactions for five years.

Bulk currency shipments continue to be an alternative for money launderers. In some cases, U.S. dollars are smuggled in bulk across the Canadian border, where they are deposited into local accounts from which they may then be wire-transferred virtually anywhere in the world.

Canada and the United States have a tradition of close cooperation on law enforcement matters, and these neighbors signed an asset seizure agreement in March 1995 that provides for mutual asset sharing in joint investigations. In addition, Canada and the United States have a mutual legal assistance treaty and a customs mutual assistance agreement. Canada has seized record amounts of currency in successive years, but actual forfeitures are negligible by comparison because of laws requiring proof of a direct link between seized property or currency and specific drug transactions.

Caribbean Dependent Territories

(High.) This section is basically a summary on Anguilla, the British Virgin Islands, Cayman Islands, Montserrat, and the Turks and Caicos Islands because notwithstanding their responding to a common policy, they have different degrees of vulnerability. The numerous offshore facilities in each island group may be abused by drug traffickers to launder money, although in recent years the United Kingdom has taken steps to tighten regulatory regimes and improve the quality of regulation in all of the territories.

Guidelines have been issued for new bank licenses, restricting such licenses to subsidiaries of established banks with effective home supervision. Given its tight secrecy laws and large offshore banking sector, the Cayman Islands are considered especially vulnerable to money launderers, particularly moving proceeds from the United States. The United Kingdom has extended the 1988 U.N. Convention to all of the territories, and each is subject to the U.S.-U.K. mutual legal assistance and extradition treaties. Each of the territories, led by the Caymans, is working on an all-crimes money-laundering statute to emulate recent British legislation. All of the territories are introducing "gateway" provisions in their financial services legislation to facilitate regulatory cooperation and to provide greater transparency with respect to beneficial ownership. Finally, as a further cooperative step, the United Kingdom is tentatively planning to move the Dependent Territories regional crime intelligence system from Tortola, British Virgin Islands, to Miami to facilitate increased liaison with U.S. agencies. This follows the on-going joint U.S.-U.K. white collar crime team established in 1995 when Scotland Yard stationed an officer in Miami to work with the FBI.

The Cayman Islands have set the pace in the Caribbean for legislation complying with the 1988 U.N. Convention and other international standards, and in 1995 adopted laws complying with convention standards on asset seizure and forfeiture and control of chemicals. A dependent territory of the United Kingdom, the Caymans had already adopted mandatory reporting of suspicious transactions, controls on international transfers of currencies, and other banking reforms following its criminalization of drug money laundering. The Caymans have also increased regulation of mutual funds and the insurance sector. Still, the Caymans are one of the largest offshore financial service centers and remain attractive to money launderers because of their sophisticated banking services, a tradition of bank secrecy, and the ease with which shell companies can be created. Shell companies are believed to play a significant role in Cayman Islands money laundering; there are an estimated 26,000 companies, along with several hundred banks, and, therefore, they cannot be closely monitored given Caymans resources. Much of the money entering the Caymans is believed to originate in the United States, and Cayman authorities cooperate closely with U.S. officials.

Channel Islands and the Isle of Man
(Medium.) The Channel Islands (Jersey and Guernsey) and the Isle of Man are major tax havens. Offshore banking is their major industry. Money laundering is a criminal offense as it relates to drug proceeds, and banks are required to report suspicious transactions. Local laws also provide for asset seizure and forfeiture, as well as asset sharing. The islands' banking systems are considered attractive to money launderers and are vulnerable, given that the great majority of money is received by wire transfers and that large sums of money are sent to North and South American as well as European destinations. Local authorities cooperate closely with DEA in identifying possible traffickers and conducting investigations.

Chile
(Medium.) New counternarcotics and anti-money-laundering laws went into effect in October 1995, a year after passage. The initial legislation was invalidated by the Supreme Court because of

constitutional issues related to asset forfeiture. The Chilean anti-money-laundering task force began operations shortly thereafter.

The question about Chile, as with numerous other governments with new anti-money-laundering laws, is how vigorously the government will implement these measures. This question is especially pertinent in Chile's case, given the dual aspect of a robust economy that has the potential to attract drug dollars as well as legitimate investment and a banking sector that is opposed to any incursions into bank secrecy.

As the law is currently written, money laundering is illegal only if the suspect financial transaction can be tied to drug proceeds. No estimates are available on the volume of illicit proceeds from other criminal activity. No evidence exists to indicate corruption of senior public officials as related to narcotics.

It is not yet clear whether the new law will ensure the availability of records to the United States or other governments. This law has yet to be tested in the court system. Measures to open the veil of bank secrecy are under consideration but not widely supported by the public or private sector.

The new law allows banks to report suspicious activities, but it does not require them to do so. Because of the newness of the law, it is uncertain whether bankers and others are protected by law with respect to their cooperation with law enforcement entities. On one hand, the law attempts to protect sources of information, but on the other hand, it tries to protect law-abiding businesses and investors from false accusations.

Chile has cooperated in a limited manner with the United States in investigating financial crimes. Financial records are difficult to obtain without a court order. The new counternarcotics law does not provide for the seizure and forfeiture of narcotics-related assets, but the law does provide for fines, imprisonment, revocation of professional licenses, and temporary closing of places of business.

China

(Medium.) China is not yet a major money-laundering country whose activities in that sector affect the United States. Chinese officials are aware of, and concerned about, the possibility that some investors in China may be engaged in money laundering. There is no money-laundering law per se in China, but Chinese officials cite a law that prohibits the covering up of the source of assets and laws against fraud as also covering money-laundering offenses. Officials are very concerned about increasing economic crimes and illicit flows of money across borders, and have sought to strengthen both international ties and regulatory efforts. Chinese officials appear to be receptive to FATF information and recommendations. They have received four FATF delegations in less than two years and have actively participated in FATF's Asian seminars. However, China has not adopted FATF recommendations into law.

Colombia

(High.) Money laundering is a natural corollary of the cocaine trade in Colombia. Law 190, enacted in June 1995, makes money laundering a crime, not limited to the proceeds of drug trafficking, but inadequate regulation of the financial industry continues to facilitate laundering of narcotics profits and investments in legitimate business. The legislation must be strengthened and adequately enforced; the legislation alone has no deterrent value, and traffickers continue to collect and enjoy their illegal profits. Colombia must prosecute money launderers, shut down their operations, and institutionalize anti-money-laundering efforts. Colombian financial institutions engage in currency transactions involving international narcotics trafficking proceeds that include significant amounts of U.S. currency. Money laundering occurs both in the banking and nonbanking financial system (e.g., exchange houses, travel agencies) and contraband, real estate, and front companies.

Law 190 stipulates a penalty of three to eight years in prison for any person who "conceals, insures, transforms, invests, transfers, keeps in his custody, transports, administers, buys the material objects of a crime or the proceeds thereof, or makes such property or assets appear to be legal." Article 31 sets the sentence at four to twelve years if the value of the properties, the material object of the crime, or the proceeds thereof, exceeds 1,000 monthly salaries (approximately U.S.$1.4 million). It also prescribes an increased penalty of one-half to three-fourths of the proceeds for cases involving kidnapping, extortion, or drug violations; if a foreign monetary or banking exchange was used in committing the crime; if property was introduced into the Colombian customs territory; or if the crime was committed by individuals entering into a contract with individuals subject to inspection, control, or supervision by the banking superintendent.

There have been no prosecutions for money laundering in Colombia. In December 1995, the prosecutor general's office (Fiscalia) established a special unit to investigate cases under the new law. The Fiscalia initiated an investigation of the finances of the Rodriguez-Orejuela family for possible violations of money-laundering provisions.

During a 12-month period from July 1995 to June 1996, the banking superintendency has levied fines of 20 million pesos (approximately U.S.$24,000) each against five major Colombian banks for failing to report suspicious transactions and accounts. All cases involved accounts at the Cali branches of banks showing a high volume of activity involving large sums of money. The banking superintendency has stated that it intends to conduct more investigations of this nature, but that its personnel lack the technical expertise to analyze complex transactions and movement of funds. The superintendency has inquired into the possibility of U.S. training assistance. The Fiscalia and the banking association agreed in December 1995 on a mutual training program on legal and financial aspects of money laundering.

Colombia's exchange control system requires that all financial institutions file reports on cash transactions exceeding U.S.$10,000, present a record of such transactions to the superintendent of banks every three months identifying the customers involved, and notify the authorities of suspicious activities. Bankers and others are protected by law with respect to their cooperation with law enforcement entities. Despite this protection, however, some bankers claim that failure to report is based partly on fear of reprisal from the narcotics traffickers. Colombia's financial statute requires due diligence and reporting to the banking superintendency, while the new anticorruption statute requires reporting to the Fiscalia and imposes criminal sanctions on bankers. Although some banks have been fined, no bankers have been prosecuted.

Colombia has not, through specific legislation or policy, addressed the problem of international transportation of illegal-source currency and monetary instruments. However, laws regulating the international wire transfer of funds apply, and there are controls limiting the amount of currency that can be brought into the country, but that law differentiates between citizens and foreigners.

Colombia has not adopted laws or regulations that ensure the availability of adequate records of narcotics investigations to appropriate U.S. personnel and those of other governments. Although Colombia is a signatory to the 1988 U.N. Convention and has adopted formal articles of ratification, due to reservations in such key areas as extradition, asset forfeiture, and money laundering, Colombia is not considered to be in compliance. Money-laundering controls are applied to nonbanking financial institutions, but enforcement in this area is weak. The Colombian National Police has cooperated with U.S. enforcement agencies on narcotics-related matters within the constraints imposed by internal resources and capabilities—but also the constraints inherent in a lack of legal authority (partly corrected by the 1995 law), the restraints on evidence sharing, and the restraints implicit in the uncertainties about the Colombian judicial process.

Colombia has not yet established effective systems for identifying, seizing, and forfeiting narcotics-related assets. The Colombian government signed an MOU with the United States in July 1990, which is the basis for the United States' being able to transfer assets forfeited in the United States with the assistance of Colombia. But the asset seizure and forfeiture provisions embodied in Law 30 of 1974 (amended in 1986) are inadequate. Colombia promised passage of stronger asset seizure and forfeiture legislation during 1995 but did not fulfill the promise. Obstacles in passing such legislation include the efforts made by narcotics traffickers to suborn and intimidate legislators. Under the current law, property rights are forfeited only if the individual is convicted of a crime or if the owner does not legally defend those rights within a year after being summoned. However, Colombia's inability to compile evidence and to prosecute and convict defendants on criminal charges brings into question the validity of the entire process. Few cases result in conviction. There are also legal loopholes that allow traffickers and others to shield assets. In practice many assets are seized, but few are forfeited. The following assets can be seized and forfeited pursuant to judicial action: instruments of crime (e.g., conveyances used to transport narcotics), farms on which illicit crops are grown, and intangible property (e.g., bank accounts). To date, no business has been seized permanently as a consequence of being used to launder drug money or other criminal proceeds.

In December 1995, the Colombian Senate passed a bill with an amendment (the so-called *narco-mico*) that would have made prosecution for the crime of illicit enrichment virtually impossible and would have effectively derailed ongoing illicit enrichment cases. The Camara (lower house) unanimously rejected the amendment; however, the Colombian Senate may attempt to reintroduce such a measure. Even in the absence of the narco-mico, conviction for illicit enrichment is nearly impossible. To date no such conviction for narcotics-related illicit enrichment has been achieved. Legislative attempts spurred by narcotraffickers to water down laws are not uncommon, and various politicians and legislators have attempted to modify or abolish the regional "faceless" justice system, which provides prosecutors or judges with anonymity.

The Colombian bankers association has declared its support for money-laundering countermeasures. The banking community cooperates with enforcement efforts to trace funds and seize bank accounts to some extent. However, there is still general reluctance to be forthcoming. Traffickers have taken retaliatory actions, in the form of legislative challenges and threats to and intimidation of Colombian officials, related to money-laundering investigations, government cooperation with the United States, and seizures of assets.

Costa Rica

(Medium-high.) Money laundering remains a serious problem in this busy banking center, giving rise to both mercurial accounts and fraudulent schemes. Costa Rica has yet to fully address the challenge posed by money-laundering activity. Some launderers smuggle funds into the country and convert them into Costa Rican currency before depositing them into bank accounts. In the past, others, posing as entrepreneurs, apparently laundered dollars through purchases of tax payment certificates, which were designed to promote exports. Although these certificates are no longer being issued, there is suspicion that revenues from drug trafficking are finding their way into real estate and tourism developments. Recent liberalization of the banking system facilitates money laundering by allowing virtually unrestricted exchange of the Costa Rican colon at near-market rates through commercial banks and certain other financial institutions. No allegations have arisen regarding encouragement, facilitation, or involvement of senior officials in money laundering.

In 1995, Costa Rica established a national money-laundering commission comprising officials from government ministries and the banking sector. The government is considering amendments to this law to incorporate the CICAD Model Regulations with appropriate changes to avoid constitutional problems. Officials are also considering changes to laws governing banking secrecy and access to information. Costa Rica has joined CFATF and ratified various international accords on money laundering.

Costa Rican law establishes drug-related money laundering as a criminal offense. Prosecutors, however, must prove that a defendant knew the funds came from drug trafficking, thereby making convictions difficult. Nonetheless, a Costa Rican court convicted drug trafficker Ricardo Alem of a 1988 money-laundering offense in April 1995 after several trials. Banking secrecy exists, but courts may order national banks to reveal information on specific accounts. Laws require banks to maintain records, report suspicious transactions, and file large-cash-transaction reports.

Costa Rica has not yet signed bilateral agreements to share in the proceeds of successful money-laundering or narcotics-trafficking investigations. It has also passed legislation and implemented regulations to facilitate the freezing and seizure of assets. The National Drug Council, under the Ministry of Justice, enforces Costa Rica's asset seizure law. The council is scrupulous in ensuring that the assets of traffickers are seized and either sold or put at the disposal of drug-related enforcement entities.

Côte D'Ivoire

(Low-medium.) Côte D'Ivoire is an important financial center in West Africa. To the extent that money laundering occurs, a significant portion is related to narcotics proceeds and involves the banking system. Illicit activities are primarily related to heroin and cocaine, and money-laundering proceeds are typically foreign owned, rather than owned by local trafficking organizations. The government's financial institutions do not engage in currency transactions involving international narcotics-trafficking proceeds that include significant amounts of U.S. currency or currency derived from illegal drug sales in the United States.

There is no formal mechanism for exchanging adequate records covering narcotics investigations and proceedings. Nonetheless, to the extent feasible, Côte D'Ivoire has indicated a willingness to respond favorably to any request. The government has not adopted any laws or regulations that ensure the availability of adequate records of narcotics investigations to appropriate U.S. personnel and those of other governments. Côte D'Ivoire is a signatory to the 1988 U.N. Convention and has adopted the formal articles of ratification, but it has not entered into any bilateral agreements with any countries for the purpose of exchanging information on money laundering.

Money laundering from drug and non-drug crimes is a criminal offense in Côte D'Ivoire. Banks are required to maintain records on large currency transactions, to report the data to the government, and to maintain for an adequate time the records necessary to reconstruct significant transactions through financial institutions. Bankers are protected by law with respect to their cooperation with law enforcement entities. Côte D'Ivoire has, to date, not been formally requested to cooperate with any law enforcement agency of the United States in investigating financial crimes related to narcotics, nor has it addressed the problem of international transportation of illegal-source currency and monetary instruments. There are controls on the amount of currency which can be brought into and out of Côte D'Ivoire. Individual bankers are not accountable for the activities of their institutions. Money-laundering controls are not applied to nonbanking institutions, and there have been no recent arrests or prosecutions for money laundering.

Cuba

(Low-medium.) Cuba's growing tourist trade, its aggressive pursuit of foreign investment, the establishment in Cuba during 1995 of several foreign banks, and its procedures for purchasing materials barred by the U.S. trade embargo through third countries like Panama provide a potential framework for significant money-laundering operations. Should Cuba permit the establishment of shell corporations and protected bank accounts so as to compete with its neighbors, it could attract substantial sums of licit and illicit funds.

However, at present, the Cuban peso is not accepted in international markets, and Cuba is not considered an important financial center in the Caribbean region. There is little evidence to support or refute Cuba's claim that no corruption, including money laundering, occurs in Cuba. The exact quantity of U.S. dollars in Cuba is unknown.

The Cuban penal code has no specific provision making money laundering a criminal offense. Section 4 of Article 190 of the code states that anyone who "helps or assists" drug offenders is subject to the same sentence as the offender. There are no known requirements for banks to report large currency transactions or other suspicious transactions. There were no reported arrests or prosecutions for money laundering during 1995. Cuba has no specific system for seizing and forfeiting assets derived from international narcotics trafficking, although the government regularly seizes and retains property suspected of being connected with illegal activity.

The lack of preventive action by the Cuban government and the potential for abuse prompt its inclusion in the low-medium category—a country to be watched.

Cyprus

(Medium-high.) Despite passage of anti-money-laundering and asset seizure laws, Cyprus is of increasing concern to the

THE ART AND SCIENCE OF MONEY LAUNDERING

United States as a center for laundering proceeds from a range of serious crimes, not limited to drug trafficking. Last year the ranking for Cyprus was raised to medium-high—a country where the United States hopes to see remedial action and countermeasures in the near future.

The certainty that performance, not just the passage of laws, is the true measure of political will is well confirmed by the situation in Cyprus. Drug money laundering is but one of the U.S. financial crime concerns that have a common root in the penetration of Cyprus by organized criminal elements. A central question, given the laws and regulations described below, is why the situation is worsening. Just three years ago, the International Narcotics Control Strategy Report (INCSR) report said that money laundering occurred outside the banking system, that Cyprus was a meeting ground where money and drugs were transferred.

Now, it is apparent that the concerns expressed in the INCSR report were well founded. There is increasing evidence of activity by Russian organized-crime groups and other criminals exploiting some of the more than 15,000 offshore companies registered on Cyprus. There is also heightened concern about the offshore banks that have been established in Turkish Cyprus and the possibility of a conduit for moving illicit funds to and from Turkey through branches of these banks in Turkey proper. Not least, there is the concern that Cypriot banks have been used to facilitate financial crimes.

Recently, the Republic of Cyprus, the southern part of the island, ratified the Council of Europe convention on "laundering, search, seizure, and confiscation of the proceeds from crime," which criminalizes money laundering from all illicit funds. Legislation to implement the convention is currently being drafted. The challenge Cyprus must confront is to implement as well as pass that legislation. Parallel with this legislative activity, cooperation between Cyprus and other countries in the field of mutual legal assistance, training, and exchange of information is likely to be significantly strengthened.

The Cypriot police force has organized a working group of financial investigators and central bank officials to identify suspicious banking transactions and accounts. The central bank requested that all banks appoint a member of their management staff as the "money-laundering compliance officer" to report suspicious transactions to the police. The central bank has also recommended that bank employees participate on an ongoing basis in special training programs to combat money laundering.

The central bank, in cooperation with the association of commercial banks, is preparing a "code of conduct" to prevent the criminal use of the banking system for the purpose of money laundering.

Restrictions on foreign ownership of property and controls on currency and bullion transiting Cyprus are among the measures that discourage efforts to launder money through the domestic economy. Cyprus law strictly controls the amount of money that residents and nonresidents can take out of the country each year. The central bank of Cyprus approves foreign currency accounts by authorized dealers and monetary activities in general. Cyprus' customs and excise department closely monitors more stringent currency declaration requirements for transiting passengers.

Cyprus has a growing offshore banking sector comprising a reported 20 banks. The central bank has supervisory powers over both sectors and has monitored large cash transfers to the offshore sector. Cypriot offshore banks may not accept foreign-currency cash deposits unless the deposits are accompanied by the appropriate customs declaration form. Over the years, the central bank has issued a series of circulars and recommendations to the financial sector, aiming to combat money laundering through the financial system. All banks in Cyprus, including domestic and offshore, have been requested to implement FATF recommendations (including know-your-customer policies). Also, all banks are to notify the central bank of any cash deposits over U.S.$10,000 in local or foreign currencies.

Czech Republic

(Medium.) Intensified concerns about the money-laundering problem prompted the recent raising of the priority for the Czech Republic from low to medium.

Money laundering in the Czech Republic had started to become a problem with the onset of (mostly) Russian organized-crime activities in the former Czechoslovakia (prior to January 1993) and the opening of the Czechoslovak economy. Recognizing its vulnerability to trafficking and money laundering, the Czech government continued vigorous police efforts against trafficking, gave police the power to conduct undercover operations, and proposed a money-laundering law.

The proposed law, introduced in November 1995, criminalized money laundering, and, in addition to the current requirement for reporting all transactions above 100,000 crowns (which would rise to 500,000 Czech crowns or about U.S.$38,000), requires banks and all other financial institutions to confirm and retain records of identification for persons conducting transactions above that level, and also requires them to report unusual transactions. A lower reporting threshold of 200,000 crowns would be required for casinos and 100,000 crowns for exchanges.

The proposed law would require reporting of cash crossing the Czech border. The Czech Republic signed the Council of Europe's convention on money laundering, seizure, and confiscation of proceeds from crime in December. As a successor to the Czech and Slovak Republic, the Czech Republic is a party to the 1988 U.N. Convention. But while the government has enacted laws authorizing asset forfeiture related to money laundering, it does not permit the sharing of funds. Similarly, banks are required to cooperate with domestic investigations, but are not permitted to cooperate with investigations by other governments.

Denmark

(Low-medium.) There are no known recent cases of money laundering in Denmark, where the laundering of both drug and non-drug-related money is a crime. Denmark has complied with FATF recommendations and requirements of the 1988 U.N. Convention.

Dominican Republic

(Medium.) The Dominican Republic is not yet an important financial center nor an important tax haven or offshore banking center. But indicators warn of its potential increased importance as a venue for money laundering. Those indications, coupled with an absence of preventive measures and enforcement actions, prompted raising its priority from low-medium to medium in 1996.

President Balaguer took a very positive step on December 18, 1995, when he signed into law amendments to the narcotics laws that establish penalties for money-laundering activities, require financial institutions to report suspicious transactions, and provide for seizure of assets derived from crime. The Bank Superintendent's Office and the National Drug Control Directorate (DNCD) are charged with enforcement of the new law. Financial institutions are now required to supply the courts, the DNCD, and other government security agencies with any information they request, as soon as possible.

Foreign-exchange transactions are legally supposed to go through the commercial banking system, but an informal process also exists for such transactions. Bank regulations have been modified to allow dollar accounts, but without further modification of the law this is not profitable. There is no provision for money laundering in the new financial monetary code. Money gained from illegal drug activities by Dominicans in the

United States is widely used to purchase or finance legitimate businesses, but there are no statistical data available about the amount. A FATF exists in name but has been powerless to act, and there have been no arrests for money-laundering-related offenses in the Dominican Republic. The Dominican Republic has been responsive to U.S. requests for information and assistance, and Dominican representatives attend CFATF meetings, but money laundering is not a criminal offense. There are no restrictions on the importation of hard currency, and up to U.S.$5,000 can be freely exported. Justifications for larger movements are not difficult to obtain. There is no law allowing for the sharing of seized assets with other countries. There are no due-diligence or banker-negligence laws. While on paper the DNCD receives proceeds and disburses them for law enforcement and prevention programs, in reality few assets are turned over by the courts. Some seized airplanes, for example, are still in the legal process after 12 years.

Shielding assets is not difficult. The DNCD court watch program now focuses only on assets in any given case. The current law allows only for criminal forfeiture. To our knowledge, traffickers have taken no retaliatory actions. There is a bank secrecy law in the country, but the superintendent of banks has full access to commercial bank records. Banks are usually willing to cooperate with law enforcement agencies.

Eastern Caribbean Overview

The decline of traditional one-crop economies and the continuing development of "offshore" financial services have enhanced the vulnerability of this region to the lure of drug money. According to 1993 estimates prepared by the Bank for International Settlements, over U.S.$5 billion of a worldwide total of $12 billion in offshore banks was placed in the Caribbean as a whole, with perhaps two-thirds as much in other offshore financial instruments. The Caribbean has long been regarded as a haven for money-laundering operations, which predate the narcotrafficking boom, but has developed in parallel with the expansion of drug trafficking and transit.

In the Eastern Caribbean, where the phenomenon is newer than elsewhere in the region, few jurisdictions have been able to develop adequate mechanisms for regulation and oversight of the offshore industry. A significant feature in 1995 was the expansion of non-drug money laundering, including from the former Soviet Union.

The heads of government of the regional organization (CARICOM) issued strong statements calling for enhanced efforts to counter money laundering. In July 1995, CARICOM prime ministers agreed on the coordination of money-laundering laws. CARICOM member states' central banks promulgated guidance notes to bankers for money-laundering prevention in June 1995. According to these guidelines, bankers are encouraged to practice due diligence in dealing with clients, keep good records, and remain vigilant for suspicious transactions. There were, however, no reports of successful prosecutions for money laundering in any of the Eastern Caribbean nations, although some countries instituted proceedings to restrain the assets of accused drug traffickers pending completion of their trials.

In 1990, the Caribbean Basin states and territories (26 jurisdictions by 1995) joined to create CFATF, a joint effort in the region modeled on the Paris-based FATF. In 1994, a secretariat was established in Port of Spain, Trinidad and Tobago, to promote anti-money-laundering measures in its members and to serve as a coordinator and focal point for donor assistance. The Caribbean region has begun to implement CFATF/FATF recommendations, which center on implementation of anti-money-laundering laws already in place. The first step, self-assessment, was performed in 1994–1995 in all 26 jurisdictions. The results, with analysis, were presented to the ministers' meeting in May 1995. Resolutions adopted included the organization of national committees on money laundering. CFATF performed mutual evaluations of the Cayman Islands, Trinidad and Tobago, and Costa Rica. CFATF assisted in the evaluation of Aruba and the Netherlands Antilles, within the context of an FATF evaluation of the Kingdom of the Netherlands.

Antigua and Barbuda

(Medium-high.) Antigua continues to be one of the more vulnerable financial centers in the Caribbean, yet its government has failed to take preventive measures. The U.S. concern about that vulnerability prompted an increase in its priority to medium-high in 1996. However, we note that the Antiguan government prepared a draft of new anti-money-laundering legislation to be submitted to its parliament, focusing on the regulation of financial institutions.

Antigua has an active offshore financial services industry, which has experienced rapid growth in recent years. In 1995, the number of offshore banks increased by about 75 percent to 42. Several of these banks have links to Russia, generating concern about investors and depositors whose funds are of unknown origin. The casino industry provides an opportunity for nonbank money laundering. Strict bank secrecy laws protect confidentiality of depositors, except in cases of violation of Antiguan law, which includes drug cases. The financial services-offshore banking industry is, in practice, unregulated. Bank licenses are freely granted by the minister of finance without the involvement of any recognized central bank. There are no mandatory reporting requirements for either large or suspicious transactions. This situation enhances the potential for abuse by those seeking to launder the proceeds of crime.

The Proceeds of Crime Act covers funds earned or received from money laundering of narcotics proceeds. One reported seizure, based on a U.S. case, may have netted the government several million dollars.

Barbados

(Low.) The offshore financial services industry continues to develop in Barbados, with particular prominence given to companies based in Canada. Because of favorable tax treaties, Barbados is characterized as a low-tax rather than no-tax jurisdiction. Government officials repeatedly assert their determination to maintain a financial industry free of taint. This was underscored at the end of 1995 in a speech by the attorney general to the hemispheric money-laundering ministerial conference in Buenos Aires, echoing a theme earlier presented to the banking community by the trade minister. Barbados signed an MLAT with the United States in August 1995.

The government keeps the financial sector under surveillance and limits tax haven privileges. In 1995, at least one financial services operator was denied permission to operate because a background check revealed a history of money laundering. Strong offshore bank laws and enforcement, backed by existing currency controls, provide a defense against the threat of laundering. Banks are expected to report large and unusual transactions voluntarily. Barbados has organized a CFATF-recommended national committee on money laundering. Sector growth will likely increase the potential for abuse.

Dominica

(No priority.) Money laundering is believed to be minimal, in part because of the underdeveloped financial sector. Some domestically-based trafficker groups launder proceeds through nonfinancial sectors of the economy. The government has ratified the 1988 U.N. Convention and criminalized money laundering. There are controls on the export of money and a requirement for banks to report unusual foreign exchange transactions.

Grenada

(No priority.) In part as a result of the limited development of the financial services industry, there is no evidence of significant money laundering.

St. Kitts and Nevis

(Low.) The announced determination of the then newly elected government in 1995 to develop a financial services industry raised the risk of money-laundering activities. Substantial trafficking through St. Kitts and trafficker activities have put this ministate at greater risk for money laundering. Some money laundering may have occurred in 1995 through the purchase of substantial real and business property. Nonetheless, the overall volume is relatively low.

St. Lucia

(Low.) Under the proceeds of the crime bill, money laundering is illegal, and there are controls on foreign exchange. Officials are adamant about protecting their banking system by ensuring adherence to offshore banking laws. There are some instances of money laundering. In 1995, a new anti-money-laundering coordination group was formed under the attorney general. The government of St. Lucia is considering steps to develop an offshore banking industry.

St. Vincent and the Grenadines

(Medium.) There have been indicators over the past year that both domestic and foreign funds earned from drug trafficking and other crimes are laundered here. Moreover, there have been allegations of corrupt payments and loans to public officials. Offshore activity is conducted without any effective regulation. Being outside the direct control of the Eastern Caribbean central banks, the offshore industry is administered only by local officials.

St. Vincent has strong laws that are in full consonance with the 1988 U.N. Convention. Authorities have cooperated, when requested, with U.S. agencies on laundering cases. In recognition of the money-laundering challenge, the government invited a U.K. financial investigating officer, who worked with the St. Vincent police from January to July 1995, to advise it on money-laundering enforcement. His efforts resulted in the freezing of approximately U.S.$300,000 in assets from a drug case awaiting trial, and a further U.S.$350,000 in the bank accounts of a second alleged drug trafficker. This work is continuing under the auspices of a British customs officer wo is contracted to train drug police and conduct financial investigations.

Ecuador
(Medium.) Although Ecuador is not considered an important financial center in its own right, it is widely viewed as a significant center for money-laundering activities, largely because of its proximity to Colombia and the close economic and social ties between the two countries. Money laundering is illegal under the 1990 narcotics law. However the law lacks specificity, stating only that it is illegal for anyone to try to hide the proceeds of drug-trafficking activity. There is no specific mention of the words "money laundering" or any comparable terminology. There is no requirement in Ecuadorian law for officials of financial institutions to exercise due diligence against money-laundering activities. Another weakness in the law is that it makes it illegal to help another party to launder money, but does not criminalize laundering one's own money. Ecuador has advised that it intends to correct this legal loophole.

Money laundering occurs in both the banking system and the nonbanking financial system. Most narcotics-related money laundering stems from the sale of cocaine, although as heroin production increases in Colombia, the percentage of money laundering due to heroin sales will undoubtedly increase as well. The great bulk of laundered money is believed to be owned by Colombians. Estimates of the annual value of money laundered in Ecuador are considered to be in the hundreds of millions of dollars. Ecuador has signed an agreement with the United States to share information on currency transactions over $10,000, but the agreement has not yet been tested. In late 1994, the superintendent of banks issued new instructions to all banks requiring them to keep internal records on the identity of persons engaging in these large transactions. The National Drug Council issued instructions to all Ecuadorian financial institutions in late 1995 requiring them to file regular reports on individuals engaging in large transactions. The information will be stored in a computerized data bank and then be readily available for sharing with the police and the United States under the terms of the bilateral agreement.

Ecuador has ratified the 1988 U.N. Convention, cooperates with the United States on money-laundering investigations, and has received from the United States assets seized with its assistance from Ecuadorian narcotraffickers. The government intends to issue instructions requiring all persons entering or leaving Ecuador to declare any negotiable monetary instruments above a certain amount; however, there would be no limit on the value of these instruments that could be transported.

The Ecuadorian association of private banks has drafted its own manual on banking procedures to prevent money laundering. There are different points of view about the liability of bankers who report suspicious transactions, but bankers often cite the potential for being sued for moral defamation as one reason for not reporting suspicious transactions. Several banks maintain offshore offices, but these have come under closer regulation under the 1994 banking reform legislation. Casas de cambio and other financial institutions are equally controlled under the banking regulations.

Ecuadorian law permits the government to temporarily seize practically all assets belonging to narcotraffickers, as well as those assets legally held by other persons where the government of Ecuador can make a credible case that the assets actually belong to the trafficker. The banking community has cooperated in several such cases, beginning with the Reyes-Torres arrest in 1992 and as recently as the Edgar Sisa case in 1995.

El Salvador

(No priority.) El Salvador has ratified the 1988 U.N. Convention. The United States is not aware of any significant money-laundering activity.

Egypt

(Low-medium.) There are no anti-money-laundering laws in Egypt, which is still trying to attract hard-currency deposits. Egypt, which is not an important financial center in the region, has not addressed the problem of the international transportation of illegal-source currency and monetary instruments. There are no controls on the amount of currency that can be brought into or out of Egypt. Individual bankers are not held responsible if their institutions launder money. However, the government reportedly continues to study amendments to improve the monitoring and investigation of suspect funds.

Estonia

(Low.) Authorities profess serious concern about financial crimes, especially money laundering, as Estonia's role as a regional financial center grows. Law enforcement officials recognize that they are ill prepared to deal with sophisticated financial crimes. Beyond seeking additional training for police, the government has still to enact laws that make money laundering an offense.

Ethiopia

(No priority.) There is no evidence that Ethiopia's archaic banking system is used for money laundering.

Finland

(Low.) A major development in Finland in 1994 was the criminalization of money laundering, thereby making this an illegal and punishable act. Significant strides toward effective use of this legislation as a basis for prosecutions were made in 1995. Finnish officials believe that little money laundering takes place in Finland.

France

(Medium.) France's asset seizure law is considered one of the strongest in Western Europe. Money-laundering legislation pending in the National Assembly will strengthen criminal penalties for money laundering and further expand authority to seize, secure, and share assets. Undercover work by police and customs officers is permitted in money-laundering cases but is used very selectively. Some U.S. law enforcement techniques, such as "sting" operations, are legal, but have not been widely accepted or employed.

A finance ministry office conducts initial investigations of suspicious bank activities; it refers money-laundering cases to a magistrate for subsequent referral to the police or customs for more extensive investigations. Before cases are referred to a magistrate, however, there must first be established at least a possible connection to drug activity. Some money laundering takes place in the French Caribbean, and drug proceeds may enter the French banking system through Caribbean branches. St. Martin, in particular, is considered a site for money laundering.

French West Indies

(Low.) Martinique, Guadeloupe, and French Guiana are départements of France, subject to French law. Money launderers are active in the islands, especially on the French side of St. Martin and on St. Barthélemy, which are part of the Guadeloupe département. The free port status, offshore banking, heavy flow of tourists, and easy access to the less-controlled Dutch half of St. Martin make that island the most susceptible to money laundering. Additional money-laundering legislation, including strengthened criminal penalties and authority to seize and share assets, was enacted in 1996. Drug proceeds enter the French banking system through branches in the Caribbean.

Georgia
(No priority.) There is no anti-money-laundering legislation in place, but the small scale of the economy and lack of an effective electronic bank transfer and clearing system make it unlikely that Georgia will become significant in this area.

Germany
(High.) Money laundering in Germany involves narcotics proceeds as well as proceeds from other illegal activities. Two significant cooperation cases between DEA and the German government have highlighted the increased use of Germany as a money-laundering center by international drug-trafficking organizations. Money laundering occurs in both the banking system and the nonbanking financial system, and money-laundering proceeds are controlled by both local and international organizations. According to press accounts, money laundering has increased to approximately DM 80 billion (U.S.$57 billion) annually. Banks appear to the main medium of exchange; lawyers and tax accountants are also involved.

German authorities have taken several initiatives to curb this activity, including new legislation, while also seeking cooperation from other governments. There are reports of German financial institutions being used for currency transactions involving international narcotics-trafficking proceeds that include significant amounts of U.S. currency and currency derived from illegal drug sales in the United States. Germany has cooperated with law enforcement agencies of the United States and other governments investigating financial crimes related to narcotics; for example, German and U.S. authorities have identified suspicious accounts and cooperated in obtaining further background information on the account holders.

Money laundering is a criminal offense (both drug-related and other-crime-related money laundering). Banks and other financial institutions are required to know, record, and report the identity of customers engaging in significant, large currency transactions. These institutions are required to maintain records necessary to reconstruct significant transactions through financial institutions to respond quickly to information requests from appropriate government authorities in narcotics-related cases. Germany requires that financial institutions report transactions of more than DM 20,000 (approximately U.S.$14,300) to state central authorities. The banking community cooperates with enforcement efforts. Bankers are protected by law with respect to cooperation with law enforcement entities. There are no controls on the amount of currency that can be brought into or out of Germany. Money-laundering controls are not applied to some nonbanking financial institutions, such as exchange houses. The controls, however, are applied to other financial institutions, such as insurance companies.

The government has the authority to forfeit seized assets, and the law allows for civil and criminal forfeiture. But other than normal inventory procedures, Germany has not established separate systems for identifying, tracing, freezing, seizing, and forfeiting narcotics-related assets; nor has it enacted laws for sharing seized narcotics assets with other governments; nor is new legislation being considered. The obstacles to passing such laws are political. Weaknesses in reporting requirements may allow traffickers to shield assets.

The drug-related asset seizure and forfeiture laws that exist are enforced by the government. Numerous German government entities are responsible for enforcement, including state prosecuting attorneys and the customs department. The police have adequate resources to seize assets. The exact value of all assets seized by all entities in all states is unknown. German authorities cooperate with U.S. efforts to trace or seize assets, and the government makes use of tips from enforcement officials in other countries regarding the flow of drug-derived assets. National laws do not permit sharing of forfeited assets with other countries.

Ghana

(Low.) Ghana reportedly experiences some money laundering, believed to be proceeds of sales of cocaine and heroin. Money laundering is a criminal offense, not limited to drug-trafficking proceeds. Banks and financial institutions are required to report large currency transactions of customers who come under investigation by law enforcement authorities. Banks are required to maintain records to reconstruct significant transactions to respond quickly to requests from appropriate government authorities in narcotics-related cases but are not required to report suspicious transactions. Data is reported only upon request by a central authority. Bankers are protected by law if requested to cooperate with law enforcement entities. There are controls on currency amounts brought into and out of the country. Ghana has established systems to identify, trace, freeze, seize, or forfeit narcotics-related assets. In October 1994, Ghana and its UNDCP subregional neighbors put into place a multilateral agreement to harmonize efforts regarding asset tracing and seizure.

Gibraltar

(Medium.) After months of intense pressure from the United Kingdom, Gibraltar passed the Criminal Justice Ordinance, which is intended to ensure that its offshore banks conform to the European Union's money-laundering directive. Gibraltar disputes Spain's contentions about the volume of money laundering on the Rock of Gibraltar, and the head of Gibraltar's Financial Services Commission contends that the new law will have little effect because the banks have always been well supervised and regulated. In mid-December 1995, a money-laundering squad was established as the central authority for receiving suspicious transactions information, and is led by a London-based metropolitan police officer.

Greece

(Medium.) In August the Greek parliament approved a law supplementing existing legislation that outlawed all forms of money laundering. The law creates various enforcement mechanisms and proof-of-identity requirements and permits controlled delivery of narcotics for enforcement purposes. Greece is not currently considered a major financial or money-laundering center. However, Greece remains vulnerable to money laundering because purchasers of government debt issues receive tax-free income, and, if the issues are paid for in cash, they are not subject to identity requirements; the sale of Greek treasury obligations now amounts to about U.S.$22.5 billion annually, or one-quarter of Greece's gross national product. In addition, seven new casinos (convenient vehicles for money laundering) were licensed in Greece in 1995.

Guatemala

(Medium.) The potential for money laundering in Guatemala is very high because of the lack of either effective monitoring and control of financial transactions or of laws specifically designed to combat money laundering. The amount of drug money being laundered through Guatemala is difficult to determine, given the lack of controls; however, current investigations indicate that money laundering is increasing. Financial institutions in Guatemala are highly vulnerable to the illicit introduction and movement of currency among Guatemala, the United States, and offshore banks. During the last year, the Guatemalan government has made little progress on criminalizing money laundering or investigating financial cases.

Guyana

(No priority.) Guyana has no laws governing money laundering, nor is there evidence that any significant volume of money laundering occurs. The Guyana attorney general has said that a new financial institutions act will include anti-money-laundering legislation.

Haiti

(Low.) Haiti is not considered an important financial center, tax haven, or offshore banking center, and the country's weak legal system, poor telecommunications, and uncertain political climate are not attractive to money launderers. Still, a substantial amount of U.S. currency enters Haiti, through the banking system and exchange houses, in the form of remittances from Haitian emigrants. This market is informal and largely cash based, and may offer opportunities for money laundering. The foreign ministry has asked relevant ministries to draft legislation on money laundering.

Honduras

(Low.) The conditions exist for major money-laundering activities as a result of the lack of legal control, but the actual extent of laundering is unknown. It is almost certain that some laundering based on cocaine transit occurs in the non-bank financial system, with such investments as hotels, supermarkets, and real estate used as vehicles for laundering. The recent passage of banking reform legislation strengthened surveillance by banks of potential laundering, and the passage of comprehensive money-laundering legislation in 1997 will significantly aid law enforcement efforts. Honduras enacted an asset seizure law in 1993 and seized a few trucks in 1994. Additional asset forfeiture legislation is currently pending in the Honduran congress.

Hong Kong

(High.) The colony's well-developed and extensive international financial networks—along with its proximity to major drug-producing countries in Asia—make it an attractive base for money-laundering activity. Low taxation rates, simple procedures for company registration, and the absence of controls on the amount of money that can enter and leave the territory adds to Hong Kong's attractiveness to money launderers. Hong Kong government authorities recognize that the territory's reputation as a financial center depends, in part, on its willingness to take effective action against money laundering activities, both drug related and otherwise. Through amendments to existing legislation, detailed elsewhere in this report, Hong Kong authorities have closed many loopholes previously exploited by traffickers. In addition, broadened bilateral cooperation on money-laundering cases is one of the objectives in negotiating a U.S.-Hong Kong MLAT. Finally, Hong Kong has implemented most of the 40 recommendations issued by FATF aimed at improving the local legal and financial framework for combating money laundering and for improving international counternarcotics cooperation.

Money laundering is a criminal offense under both the Drug Trafficking (recovery of proceeds) Ordinance and the Organized and Serious Crimes Ordinance. Reporting of suspicious financial transactions to the Joint Financial Intelligence Unit (a joint police and customs and excise department unit) is an explicit legal obligation of financial institutions under the ordinances. No mandatory reporting requirements exist for deposits over a specific amount. Rather, guidelines issued by the Hong Kong monetary authority require institutions to observe specific standards and procedures for recordkeeping and customer identification, and to pay special attention to all complex, unusually large transactions.

Hong Kong police had reported in September 1995 that in the previous two years the number of suspicious transactions had "shot up 15 times." Records must be kept for six years, and those pertaining to ongoing investigations or that have been subject to disclosure are required to be retained until the pertinent case is closed. In an effort to ensure that banking institutions are prudently managed, Hong Kong's banking ordinance requires Hong Kong monetary authority approval for all chief executives (including alternates) and bank directors of institutions incorporated in Hong Kong.

The operations of remittance centers and other nonbank institutions in the territory are of growing concern, both to U.S. and Hong Kong authorities. There is no existing legislation to regulate these nonbank entities—primarily money changers or lenders and pawnbrokers—and there is evidence that drug proceeds are increasingly being channeled through these nonregulated avenues. Hong Kong authorities have identified the creation of a regulatory framework for remittance centers as a high priority. Now that Hong Kong has reverted to China, the measures to be taken in this former British colony against money laundering will be examined in light of its new political status.

Hungary

(Medium.) Hungary is neither a major regional financial center nor a tax haven. Money laundering has been illegal since 1994, and banks are required to report significant cash transactions regularly. In light of poor internal banking controls, some money laundering probably occurs, but narcotics traffickers are not particularly active.

Banks and other financial institutions are required to know, record, and report the identity of individuals and companies conducting large currency transactions and to maintain records on such transactions. Data are reported to the ministry of finance. Hungary cooperates with U.S. law enforcement agencies on the financial aspects of narcotics-related crime. Asset forfeiture laws exist but are not applied in practice. Hungary and the United States signed an MLAT in 1994.

Iceland

(No priority.) Iceland has not ratified the 1988 U.N. Convention but does have anti-money-laundering regulations derived from the European Economic Agreement. Between September and December 1994, a Bahamian-registered company laundered about $10 million through two Icelandic commercial banks. A woman was arrested in Belgium in connection with this scheme, which was not narcotics related. Authorities attribute the success of the detection and prosecution of this case to Iceland's regulations on money laundering, the small size of its banking system, the novelty of large capital flows, and the government's desire to maintain Iceland's good name.

India

(Medium-high.) Although money laundering is not a criminal offense per se, those suspected of hiding funds can be prosecuted for income tax evasion under the Income Tax Act, with penalties of up to seven years' imprisonment. Under- or overinvoicing, two common ways of hiding drug money, are offenses and can be prosecuted under customs law. India has set up a committee to look into drafting specific money-laundering legislation, but to date, no proposals have gone forward. Anyone establishing a bank account must provide a photograph of himself, and transactions over RS 50,000 (U.S.$1,470) cannot be made in cash. All transactions over RS 100,000 (U.S.$2,940) must be reported to bank management, which then decides whether to notify the authorities.

The government has issued administrative instructions to financial institutions to report suspicious transactions, but they are under no legal obligation to do so. Bankers are protected by law when they cooperate with law enforcement authorities. When requested, India has cooperated with U.S. law enforcement agencies and those of other countries. There are controls on the amount of currency that can be brought into or taken out of the country. Foreigners must declare amounts in excess of U.S.$10,000; Indians must declare the rupee equivalent of U.S.$10,000. The government has not adopted due-diligence laws that make individual bankers responsible if their institutions launder money.

Under the Narcotic Drugs and Psychotropic Substances Act of 1985, amended in 1989, illegally acquired property can be frozen or forfeit. This law applies only to the assets of those persons actually convicted of crimes, however, which enables those who have been arrested to hide their assets before conviction. The government hopes to broaden this act to apply to those who have been arrested or against whom a warrant has been issued. There are no political obstacles to passing a tougher law, but the overlapping jurisdiction of several ministries has slowed the process.

Under the act, instruments of crimes (such as laboratories) are immediately forfeit, although the actual farms on which illegal crops are grown are not. Any asset acquired through illegal proceeds can be forfeit. Legitimate businesses that launder money cannot be seized. The national fund for control of drug abuse receives the proceeds from narcotics-related asset seizures and forfeitures. The courts can forfeit assets if they are an instrument of offense. If the assets are acquired from the proceeds of a crime, a competent authority has the power to forfeit them. Competent authorities include officials of the state police, state drug control agencies, Forest Department, Central Customs, Central Excise, the Central Bureau of Investigation, the Narcotics Control Bureau, and the Central Bureau of Narcotics. Even though these authorities have sufficient powers, resources are inadequate and, with the exception of the Narcotics Control Bureau and Central Bureau of Narcotics, they have other mandates to fulfill as well, which may take priority. As of July 1995, U.S.$1.3 million of assets were frozen, and U.S.$1.6 million of assets were forfeited, which is an increase from the previous year. India is open to efforts by the United States and other countries to trace and seize assets, and it makes use of tips from other countries. The government has bilateral narcotics agreements with 10 other countries, but the focus is not on asset seizure. National laws do not permit the sharing of forfeited assets with other countries. The banking community has been fairly cooperative, but bank secrecy laws are not strict in any case.

Indonesia

(Low.) Although Indonesia is not a major producer of narcotics or a money-laundering center, it is increasingly used as a transit point for Southeast Asian heroin, including transshipment to the United States, Australia, and Europe. As interdiction efforts increase in other countries, use of Indonesia as a transshipment point is expected to escalate. Indonesia's booming economy has created greater links to international markets, including increased air connections to the United States and expansion of international shipping. Indonesia's tourism boom has increased the incidence of narcotics trafficking, particularly in Bali. The nation's criminal code lists a limited number of illicit narcotics and does not include prohibitions. Indonesia has not passed anti-money-laundering laws of any kind. It has signed but not ratified the 1988 U.N. Convention.

Ireland

(Low.) Ireland is not a significant financial center, tax haven, or offshore banking center, and the government is unaware of any systematic money-laundering activities. The government of Ireland, as a matter of policy, works to discourage money laundering through significant criminal penalties enacted in the 1994 Criminal Justice Act, which made drug-related money laundering a criminal offense when it came into effect in May 1995. In the period that this legislation has been in effect two cases have been referred for prosecution by the director of public prosecutions. Irish law does not permit sharing of forfeited assets with other governments. The customs service and the national police regularly confiscate conveyances used to transport narcotics, usually cars and trucks. These vehicles are retained by the confiscating agency or used by other government agencies as official vehicles. Ships that have been seized become the property of the Irish Department of Defense.

Israel

(Medium-high.) The priority for Israel has recently been raised to medium-high, reflecting public statements by senior Israeli officials that Israel is emerging as an increasingly significant money-laundering center for Russian criminals. Israeli officials have stated that Israeli organized crime has processed drug proceeds through Israeli financial institutions, in Israel and abroad, using U.S. dollars. Money laundering is not yet a prosecutable crime, and benign banking laws, a policy of not taxing foreign accounts, and a lucrative stock exchange continue to make Israel an attractive investment and financial safe haven. There are no accepted figures on the scope of money laundering in Israel, but there have been estimates suggesting that the funds involved may be substantial. The Israeli government does not as a matter of policy facilitate or engage in money-laundering activities.

Israel has not adopted laws or regulations that ensure the availability of adequate records of narcotics investigations to appropriate personnel of U.S. or other governments, but Israeli law permits cooperation without a formal treaty. Proposed mutual legal assistance legislation to go before the Knesset will allow for comprehensive reciprocal legal assistance with competent foreign authorities regarding asset forfeiture investigations, the provision of material evidence and witnesses for forfeiture proceedings, the attainment of temporary injunctions

or restraining orders vis-à-vis property, and the implementation of forfeiture orders. The 1995 dual-taxation treaty
between the United States and Israel grants U.S. tax authorities
limited access to bank account information. An MLAT with
the United States remains under protracted negotiation, but
appears stalled over territorial issues and how to treat criminal
tax offenses.

Israel has signed but not yet ratified the 1988 U.N. Convention. According to the foreign ministry, the political will to ratify
the accord is there, but some issues—including Israel's prohibition
against extraditing its citizens—has not yet been resolved. Israel
has acceded to the Council of Europe Convention on mutual legal
assistance in criminal matters. It has narcotics cooperation agreements with Italy and Turkey that cover law enforcement cooperation, though not specifically about money laundering.

Israel's Ministry of Justice completed drafting money-laundering legislation and plans to table it before the Knesset. Under
current laws, money laundering is not an independently prosecutable crime; a specific criminal conviction must be obtained
before forfeiture proceedings to seize income, property, and
other "fruit of trafficking" may be instituted. This legal requirement has limited the success of law enforcement agencies in
pursuing money-laundering cases. Nonetheless, one of the priority objectives of the Israeli National Police is to follow up major
trafficking convictions with asset forfeiture proceedings.

Israeli law enforcement agencies have established an interagency commission to further the practical application of this
legislation. However, several laws make prosecuting money-
laundering cases difficult. Banking secrecy laws permit banks
to divulge information only after the proper court order has
been obtained. Moreover, there are no currency controls on
large transactions by non-Israeli citizens. Foreign residents
with local accounts, for example, are not required to file
Israeli tax returns.

Anticipating new money-laundering laws, the Israeli National Police plans to establish a small 12-person unit to receive compulsory cash reports from banks for transactions over U.S.$10,000. The unit will also receive and process declarations of cash entering and exiting Israel.

An asset forfeiture law, enacted in 1989, allows for the seizure and forfeiture of all financial assets—present and past, up to eight years—of convicted traffickers and their immediate families. The defendant carries the burden of proof to show that these assets were legally acquired and not the fruit of narcotrafficking. Legitimate businesses that launder money may be included in forfeiture proceedings only if their owners have been convicted on drug-trafficking charges. Under current Israeli law, however, a business proven by its owner to have been established with legitimate money may never be forfeited, even if the owner is convicted of drug-trafficking offenses.

All court-forfeited assets are centrally administered by a specific office in the Ministry of Justice, which may make grants of the seized funds to law enforcement agencies. The law also permits civil forfeiture of assets that were the result of, or instrumental in, the commission of drug trafficking or production. Civil forfeiture does not require a prior criminal conviction. The government enforces existing drug-related asset seizure and forfeiture legislation, and asset forfeiture has become increasingly frequent. The 1989 forfeiture law was enacted primarily because of lobbying by law enforcement agencies.

Italy
(High.) The financial sector in Italy serves as a significant money-laundering center for both narcotics and other illicit funds. The Italian banking and nonbanking systems are used by local and South American drug traffickers primarily to launder proceeds from heroin and cocaine drug activities.

The U.S.-Italy MLAT provides a mechanism for exchanging evidence in connection with narcotics investigations. Italy and the United States are exploring means to implement the now-suspended seizure and forfeiture article of the treaty or to develop alternative mechanisms. Italy has ratified the 1988 U.N. Convention and is an active participant in the FATF and the EU effort. Furthermore, Italy has numerous bilateral agreements for the exchange of information on money laundering.

Italy's 1994 comprehensive money-laundering law is fully consistent with the FATF's 40 recommendations and the EU's money-laundering directive. Italy cooperates closely with the United States on financial crimes related to narcotics, including in major joint operations such as Green Ice, Dinero, and Universal Gold. In one 1995 case, Italian authorities froze the bank accounts of accused drug trafficker José Santacruz-Londoño, in connection with a New York trial of his associates.

Italian banks were initially slow to implement all the regulations of the new law but have not publicly fought it. Italian authorities believe that implementation of the 1994 law and the success of joint operations with the United States have led some drug traffickers to conduct money laundering outside Italy.

Italy has an established system for identifying, tracing, freezing, seizing, and forfeiting narcotics-related assets. Italy is committed by Council of Europe Convention procedures for sharing such assets with other governments. There are no new laws under consideration. Under existing regulations, businesses used for money laundering can be seized, and the government has the authority to forfeit such assets. However, criminals have in some cases used family members to shield assets. Proceeds from seizures go to the Italian treasury. The law also allows for civil forfeiture of assets as a precautionary measure separate from a criminal conviction.

MONEY LAUNDERING ANALYSIS BY COUNTRY

In 1995, the Italian government seized over $1.5 billion in assets from organized crime and narcotics figures. Italy cooperates fully with the United States and other countries and exploits tips from other governments regarding the flow of drug-derived assets. It remains engaged with other governments in negotiations to harmonize asset-tracing and seizure efforts. Banks, while not actively resisting, have provided surprisingly few reports of suspicious activities to the government. Traffickers have not taken any retaliatory actions, but fear is often cited as a reason why banks—especially in the south—have made so few reports to the government.

Jamaica

(Low.) Jamaica is not a major money-laundering nation, nor an important Caribbean financial center, although the financial sector has been enjoying impressive local growth. Jamaica has ratified the 1988 U.N. Convention but has not yet adopted enabling legislation to criminalize money laundering and impose related controls. A money-laundering bill was introduced in parliament in late 1995.

Jamaica has adopted laws that ensure the availability of adequate records of narcotics investigations to appropriate U.S. personnel and those of other governments. Banks can be requested to report suspicious transactions, and bankers are protected against liability for evading bank secrecy.

However, banks and other financial institutions are not required to know, record, and report the identity of customers engaging in significant large currency transactions, nor is there a time limit for retention of records. There are no controls on the amount of currency that can be brought into or out of the country. An assets forfeiture law was passed in August 1994; it requires prior conviction for a drug offense, and the assets must be related to the offense.

Japan

(Medium-high.) Money laundering remains a criminal offense only if it is related to drug trafficking. In other key respects, Japanese law is consistent with the 1988 U.N. Convention, which it has ratified, and with FATF recommendations. Japan is the only member of the eight-member Pacific FATF, which created FATF, that has not criminalized the laundering of proceeds from all serious crimes. At a recent conference in Paris, Japan's representatives discussed extension of non-narcotic money-laundering legislation within two to three years. The Minister of Justice will act as the initiator of the new laws.

Japanese banks and financial institutions are required to report suspicious transactions and to know, record, and report the identity of customers engaging in significant large-currency transactions, and to maintain for an adequate time records necessary to reconstruct significant transactions through financial institutions to be able to respond quickly to information requests from appropriate government (foreign as well as domestic) authorities in narcotics-related cases. However, Japan has shared such information with other nations only informally.

Bankers are protected by law with respect to their cooperation with law enforcement entities. Japan has placed controls on the amount of currency that can be brought into or out of the country. It has also extended money-laundering controls to nonbank financial institutions; however, there are no reported arrests or prosecutions for money laundering.

Japan has established systems for identifying, tracing, freezing, seizing, and forfeiting narcotics-related assets, but does not share seized narcotics assets with other governments. The Japanese seizure statute allows the government to seize only those funds that can be directly linked to a specific drug investigation or violation: illicit proceeds, any property derived from illicit proceeds, any property obtained in reward for conducting an offense, any property ruled fruit of the crime. In the event that illicit funds have been commingled with legitimate funds, an amount equivalent to the illicit amount can be seized. Although seizure laws have been in place since 1989, only one money seizure has occurred to date.

Jordan
(No priority.) Jordanian officials state that money laundering is not now a major problem in Jordan but is a concern. There are no laws for financial institutions to follow and no programs in place to deal with money laundering. Local authorities know that the transportation and distribution of drugs is largely handled in cash by nomadic Bedouin tribesmen. This situation does not allow for the easy tracking of drug money. Jordan is not viewed as a major financial center for drug traffickers in the region. Foreign-exchange facilities are government regulated and directly linked to banks.

Kenya
(Low.) Kenya is East Africa's financial hub, but the country is not a significant money-laundering center. Narcotics officers in Nairobi and on the East African coast suspect, however, that Kenya's casino industry may be an avenue for narcotics-related laundering. Except for one car, Kenya has not seized any assets in connection with drug trafficking. Under the Kenyan Narcotic Drugs and Psychotropic Substances Control Act, proceeds from narcotics-related asset seizures go into a rehabilitation fund for drug addicts. Currently, Kenya does not have agreements with other countries to share seized assets or information on money laundering. The narcotic drugs law nevertheless allows the Kenyan government to provide such assistance to other countries upon request. During 1995, the central bank issued and then almost immediately withdrew a circular notice that requested banks to identify the sources of their depositors' funds

before accepting their accounts. Later, the national assembly adopted an amendment to the Central Bank Act that authorized restrictions on foreign-exchange transfers for purposes of meeting treaty obligations. The amendment also required that all payments to, from, or within Kenya be processed through authorized banks. According to the attorney general, this provision enabled the central bank to ensure that international payments were not connected with money laundering.

Korea

(Medium.) U.S. officials have had difficulty in tracing the movement of funds to specific drug shipments. However, there have been reports of Nigerians and Colombians entering Korea with thousands of U.S. dollars in bulk. Moreover, Korea is known to be a depository for funds generated by the large trade in methamphetamine that reaches from East Asia to Hawaii. Korea, which in 1995 was stung by admissions from former President Roh Tae Woo that he had deposited nearly U.S.$250 million in secret bank accounts outside his country, is taking actions to prevent financial crimes, including money laundering. Asset-seizure laws related to drug trafficking were proposed in 1995 that would allow the freezing of accounts and prevent traffickers from moving assets out of Korea, while also permitting Korea to honor foreign forfeiture orders. False-name bank accounts have been banned, and banks are required to advise the authorities of suspected drug-related deposits. However, foreign banks in Korea are not subject to the same regulations as domestic banks, and citizens can hold unlimited amounts in foreign currency accounts. Korea has a vast underground banking system whose volume is estimated at more than U.S.$32 billion annually. Although the system is not believed to be used extensively by money launderers, it may become more attractive as the banking system is regulated.

Kuwait

(Medium.) Despite a lack of hard data on money being laundered there, Kuwait remains a medium priority because of its potential as a money-laundering center, given its absence of currency controls and reporting requirements and its loosely regulated network of money exchangers, coupled with the known and assumed flows of money into and out of the country.

Kyrgyzstan

(No priority.) The Kyrgyzstan banking system is undeveloped. It is not easy to electronically transfer funds into and out of the country. It is not an attractive center for money laundering. There have been allegations that drug money has been deposited into local banks for use and then diverted into legitimate enterprises. There are no laws that specifically address money laundering. The Kyrgyztan government is more concerned with the larger problem of money from other forms of illegal activity, such as government corruption. There is no specific Kyrgyztan law on asset forfeiture. The legal basis for such action is contained in the corresponding articles of the criminal code of the former Soviet Union. If a person has been found guilty and convicted by the court, the person's property is to be confiscated, with 30 percent of the proceeds going to the law enforcement agencies.

Laos

(Low.) Laos is not considered a major financial center, and its commercial banking system is only in the early stages of development, with the assistance of international financial institution consultants. Nonetheless, the Laotian government has expressed interest in development of money-laundering legislation. Although the government welcomes foreign banks, only one Thai bank to date has begun operations in Vientiane, the Laotian capital. The draft legislation package, which was prepared by a UNDCP legal expert, includes a section on money laundering. In 1995, a Laotian banking official attended a money-laundering symposium conducted for Asian countries by FATF and hosted by the Japanese government. The Laotian kip is not a free currency, and there are very strict laws on its export.

Laotian customs legislation, enacted in 1994, specifically authorizes asset seizure in that the law states that the means of conveyance of contraband can be seized along with the contraband. The UNDCP advisor, who departed in mid-1995 after a one-year assignment to Vientiane, stated that under current laws and judicial procedure, provisions are adequate to deal with narcotics violations and that the courts can order seizure of assets. He stated, however, that additional legislation would be required should the current authoritarian system of national political administration be modified in the direction of greater individual rights, including the rights of those accused of crimes. The draft legislation noted above includes a section on asset forfeiture, which does in fact occur in Laos. A boat seized in connection with a 1994 drug case in Bokeo Province was turned over to law enforcement agencies by the court following conviction of the traffickers in 1995. In another case, a pickup truck being used to transport drugs was seized and held by police until the court ruled on the case. Customs officials were pleased that the court forfeited the property to the Laotian government since it was being used to smuggle drugs.

Latvia

(Low.) Latvia has the potential to be a money-laundering center because of its lack of effective banking regulations for its sizable banking industry. U.N. economic analysts have been assisting the Bank of Latvia on draft money-laundering legislation. The lack of anti-money-laundering legislation, the absence of strict banking accountability, and the large number of banks formed under very loose regulations could attract money launderers. A scandal involving the then largest bank in Latvia,

Banka Baltija, occurred in the spring of 1995, amid public allegations that the bank's owners and top management raided its assets prior to its closure for financial improprieties by the Latvian National Bank. Major international investigations into the affair are ongoing with the FBI and other law enforcement agencies from other countries conducting their own investigations into Banka Baltija's dealings. Despite some efforts at liaison, there still is a lack of coordination among the police, border guards, and customs officials. Low salaries and lack of proper training and equipment for these civil servants severely hamper efforts to stop illegal trafficking at the borders.

Lebanon

(Medium.) Lebanon's bank secrecy laws, which do not allow for law enforcement discovery, create an opportunity that money launderers are likely to exploit. Lebanon has ratified the 1988 U.N. Convention. In its accession, however, the legislature made reservations to the language on bank secrecy laws. Thus current bank secrecy protections, which do not allow for legitimate law enforcement concerns, foster an environment for both money laundering and corruption.

The Lebanese government has proposed legislation that will criminalize money laundering and reportedly will deal harshly with convicted money launderers. But for now, Lebanon imposes none of the measures deemed essential to combat money laundering or to ensure adequate levels of prudential supervision of banks.

Lesotho

(No priority.)

Liberia

(No priority.)

Liechtenstein

(Medium-high.) A major "offshore" banking center, Liechtenstein adopted legislation criminalizing laundering of drug proceeds in 1993 and is now preparing a more comprehensive law that will criminalize money laundering as a stand-alone offense. Pursuant to an MLAT request from the United States, Liechtenstein has blocked a bank account holding U.S.$8 million in the name of an Ecuadorian endowment fund. The government conducted its own investigation of a second account sought by the United States and located and froze another U.S.$9 million.

Lithuania

(Low.) The regulation of Lithuania's private banking sector is still in its formative stage, so the country's banks could be vulnerable to money-laundering operations. The law on commercial banking and legislation of income and assets declaration for tax purposes that was passed in 1994 helped strengthen the legal framework for fighting the drug problem. There have been no reported cases of high-level corruption associated with the drug trade.

Luxembourg

(Medium-high.) A major world financial center, hosting more than 230 international banks that operate as "universal banks" with an unrestricted range of activities, Luxembourg is a tax haven as a result of its banking secrecy laws, absence of exchange controls, lack of withholding tax on interest, and politically stable environment. However, banking secrecy does not apply in criminal cases, including money laundering.

Government officials acknowledge that narcotics money laundering occurs, but they do not consider Luxembourg more of a center for such activity than other places with highly developed banking systems. Virtually all recent money-laundering cases involve funds introduced into the world financial system elsewhere (usually from within Europe) that were then transferred to Luxembourg for layering or integration. In all money-laundering cases, Luxembourg law holds bankers personally liable if they fail to establish the bona fides of the owners who benefit from funds when they are received. The Monetary Institute has stepped up its efforts to police the banks' anti-money-laundering performance.

There have been no indications that the nonbanking financial sector has been involved in money laundering. The government continues to closely monitor nonbank institutions, such as building companies, real estate agencies, jewelry stores, art galleries, and antique dealers.

Asset forfeiture remains the focus of bilateral relations with the United States on money laundering. The Luxembourgeois government has been very active in information sharing and joint investigations with the United States and other countries. The Luxembourgeois authorities have made good use of tips provided by U.S. agencies to seize money and assets belonging to drug traffickers.

Luxembourg ratified the 1988 U.N. Convention on March 17, 1992, bringing Luxembourg's law into conformity with the convention. Luxembourg is also a member of FATF and has implemented many of its recommendations. Luxembourg is party to both the European Convention on Judicial Assistance and the BENELUX (Belgium, the Netherlands, and Luxembourg) Convention on Extradition and Assistance.

Under current Luxembourgeois legislation, only drug-related money laundering is a criminal offense. The laws will be changed once Luxembourg ratifies the Strasbourg Convention to criminalize all money laundering. Under Luxembourg's 1992 law, the punishment for money laundering is a minimum jail term of two years and a minimum fine of 10,000 Luxembourgeois francs (approximately U.S.$345).

Under Luxembourg's financial sector law of April 10, 1993, bankers and other financial dealers are required to keep documents or information on transactions for at least five years. The

1993 law also requires financial sector professionals to report suspicious transactions to the public prosecutor. Exchange dealers, lawyers, notary publics, and bankers who handle securities are under the same obligation. As stated above, the first annual report on banks' performance of the duty to report "suspicious transactions" was published in March 1995.

Bankers are criminally responsible if their institutions knowingly launder drug money. Client identity must be verified for transactions exceeding LF 500,000 (approximately U.S.$16,000 at the time of this writing). Under Luxembourg's bank secrecy law, the 1993 law protects from criminal or civil prosecution those financial professionals who in good faith provide information on clients to the authorities. There are no controls on money brought into or taken out of the country.

Luxembourgeois law provides for asset forfeiture in criminal cases, and the first forfeiture occurred in 1994. Forfeiture can follow a finding that the assets to be forfeited were involved in narcotics-related money laundering or following criminal conviction. It remains unclear whether Luxembourgeois courts will enforce civil forfeiture orders from elsewhere, because the concept of civil forfeiture does not exist in national law. In criminal matters, seized funds cannot be forfeited directly under pre-1992 law, which requires a criminal conviction in order for the money to be forfeited.

Macao

(Medium.) A special territory of Portugal's, Macao is a renowned gambling center and reputed safe haven for Hong Kong criminals. Asian organized crime and drug-trafficking groups have long been suspected of using Macao's unregulated casinos to launder money, and the banking system is considered conducive to money laundering because of strict bank secrecy laws. Any financial institution that accepts a deposit of more than U.S.$12,500 commits a crime under a 1993 law, but that law does not apply to casinos.

Macedonia

(No priority.) Although drugs are trafficked through Macedonia, the economy still operates on a largely cash basis, and the banks have only begun to restructure themselves, four years after independence from the former Yugoslavia. There is no indication of significant money laundering.

Madeira and the Azores

(Medium.) The analysis of these two regions is separate from that of the mother state, Portugal, because they are autonomous and are not subject to all Portuguese laws. Portugal is not considered a major financial center and is ranked as a low-medium priority, but Madeira and the Azores are ranked higher because of concern about offshore banking activity in both regions. Neither region imposes bank reporting requirements on its offshore banking sector.

Malaysia

(Medium.) The only legislative protection against money laundering is an asset-seizure law that makes drug-related money laundering a criminal offense. The asset seizure law is narrow in scope and has had only limited success in confiscating drug money. Senior government officers recognize the need for a stronger and broader anti-money-laundering regimen and have publicly called for implementation of measures to combat money laundering. Following the meeting of Commonwealth heads of state in Auckland last year, the deputy finance minister promised that Malaysia will make money laundering a serious crime and take action within the framework of its laws to combat such illegal activity. In this regard, the government is currently studying the draft model law for the prohibition of money laundering prepared by the Commonwealth secretariat.

Malaysia is concerned that its offshore banking center, Labuan, may become a money-laundering conduit. Although

Malaysian laws provide the police full access to bank records, experts believe that comprehensive anti-money-laundering enforcement is necessary to prevent money-laundering activities in Labuan.

Malta

(Low.) Although not currently significant as a money-laundering sector, Malta could increase its importance in this activity as other governments in Europe and around the Mediterranean tighten their banking controls and enforce money-laundering countermeasures.

Mauritius

(No priority.) A money-laundering bill was introduced in July 1995 in parliament but not acted upon, so there is no legislation against money laundering in Mauritius. As yet, only seven banks have been approved for offshore banking, including Barclays, Bank of Baroda, Hong Kong Shanghai, and Rothschilds. According to Mauritian authorities, these banks were selected because of their reputations and the internal controls they have against money laundering. The money-laundering bill was designed to comply with model legislation drafted by the FATF. Until the bill passes, however, money laundering, except as it relates to other offenses, is not a crime in Mauritius. Accordingly, there have not been arrests or seizures in connection with alleged money laundering. The offshore banking authority reports that it has stringent standards for approving offshore companies but does not have formal information-sharing agreements with authorities elsewhere. The country's role as a center for financial services and its booming tourism industry (and related high-cash-turnover restaurants and casinos) make it potentially vulnerable to illicit money-laundering activities.

Mexico

(High.) Increasingly effective measures have been taken by the United States to deter narcotraffickers' placement of drug cash into its financial system. Therefore, Mexico has become the money-laundering haven of choice for initial placement of U.S. drug cash into the world's financial system. Once placed into Mexico's financial system, these cash proceeds are being moved in a variety of forms, including wire transfers and drafts drawn on Mexican banks payable through U.S. correspondent accounts. By their own statements, Mexican officials have estimated that the amount of drug cash repatriated to Mexican drug cartels in 1994 was some $30 billion, and the total amount moved into Mexico for eventual repatriation to Colombia is much higher.

Proximity to the United States, endemic corruption, and little or no regulation or enforcement of regulations of the deposit of U.S. drug dollars in the Mexican financial infrastructure (coupled with the purging of the U.S. financial system of the initial placement of drug cash) have combined to make Mexico the number one country of choice for the movement of drug cash generated by Western Hemisphere drug cartels. A comprehensive system of legal, financial, and regulatory reforms must be passed and implemented, or the situation will only grow worse, to the economic and political detriment of both countries.

Mexico's financial institutions are being used for large U.S. dollar cash transactions derived from narcotics and non-narcotics proceeds. Ill-gotten money is laundered in both the banking and nonbanking financial systems. A number of investment firms and legitimate businesses have also been implicated in money-laundering schemes. Mexican and international narcotrafficking organizations launder proceeds in Mexico from cocaine, opiate, and cannabis trafficking. Mexico has done little to curb these practices, which are enormously profitable for Mexico's banking community and the brokers and criminals who exploit that system.

Mexican officials have stated that an important factor in their inability to curb money laundering is that Mexico's supervision and enforcement systems are permeated by suborned officials. Their goal now is to broaden and define legal sanctions against money laundering. A few former senior Mexican government officials are suspected of and have been investigated for money laundering, including Mario Ruíz Massieu (U.S.$20 million) and Raúl Salinas Gotarí (U.S.$90 million). Raúl Salinas Gotarí, brother of ex-President Carlos Salinas, transferred some U.S.$80–90 million from a branch of Citibank in Mexico City through its headquarters in New York City to a Swiss bank account. (Raúl Salinas has been indicted for conspiracy to murder.) Investigations into possible money laundering by him continue.

Former Deputy Attorney General Mario Ruíz Massieu, currently under arrest in the United States, is also under investigation in Mexico for money laundering. He has been found to have bank accounts in the United States totaling U.S.$24 million, including $9 million in Texas, funds believed to be proceeds from money laundering and payoffs for protecting narcotraffickers. He has been indicted in Mexico for embezzlement, money laundering, and unjust enrichment. Investigations into possible money laundering continue.

Mexico signed an MLAT with the United States in 1987, as well as a financial information exchange treaty with the U.S. Department of the Treasury in October 1994. Mexico has not yet adopted laws or regulations, however, to ensure the availability of adequate records of narcotics investigations to appropriate U.S. and third-nation personnel. Mexico is a signatory to the 1988 U.N. Convention, as well as the Summit of the Americas money-laundering agreement. Mexico has shown interest in joining FATF and agreed at the December 1995 Summit of the Americas Conference on Money Laundering in Argentina to participate in a money-laundering task force. Mexico has also entered into other bilateral agreements to exchange money-laundering information and share such fiscal data as tax records with Canada, France, Germany, Ecuador, Switzerland, Spain, and Italy.

U.S. and Mexican law enforcement agencies work closely together in the field of money laundering. During 1995, the Mexican Secretariat of Treasury (Hacienda) assisted the U.S. Customs Service Office of Investigations in providing referral information on seven significant money-laundering cases in Mexico. In addition, Hacienda provided U.S. Customs with information resulting in the initiation of five significant money-laundering cases in the United States. During 1995, Hacienda's money-laundering section completed 11 money-laundering investigations in Mexico and referred them to the attorney general (PGR) for prosecution. The PGR also cooperated with the DEA in several significant financial investigations during 1995. In 1995, the IRS conducted 19 joint investigations with Hacienda, which resulted in two major convictions in the United States and the seizure of nearly U.S.$1 million from the Arrellano-Felix organization. Furthermore, fiscal regulations require banks and other financial institutions to know, record, and report the identity of customers engaging in suspicious currency transactions.

The same regulations require banks and financial institutions to maintain adequate time records necessary to reconstruct significant transactions through financial institutions. Fiscal regulations for nonfinancial firms are loose, however, and are only applied when the company is audited. Financial institutions dealing in international currency transactions, on the other hand, are required to complete and maintain records for all such transactions.

Although Mexico requires financial institutions to report suspicious transactions, there are currently no penalties for failure to report. However, new mandatory penalties were written into legislation, which also provided legal protection to financial officers who cooperate with law enforcement personnel. The transportation across Mexican borders of currency in amounts greater than U.S.$10,000 must be reported to Mexican authorities.

The Ministry of Treasury's Money Laundering Directorate has cooperated with U.S. Customs and the IRS in the investigation of financial crimes related to narcotics. Major investigations conducted during 1995 include the following:

- The Mexican government provided critical information and assistance to U.S. Customs during Operation Choza Rica. The long-term investigation culminated in the seizure of a U.S.$30 million investment portfolio managed by American Express Bank International. As a result of its participation in the investigation, the United States presented Mexico with a check for more than U.S.$6 million from the seized assets.
- In the Mario Ruíz Massieu investigation, the United States was able, with Mexican government assistance, to freeze and potentially forfeit U.S.$9 million in Houston. Mexico's Secretariat of Treasury provided documentary evidence and testimony in U.S. federal court, which resulted in the conviction of the defendants and forfeiture of more than U.S.$4.5 million in drug proceeds.
- Humberto Garcia Abrego, brother of recently expelled Gulf cartel head Juan Garcia Abrego, is currently serving a five-year sentence in a Mexican federal prison after being charged with laundering drug proceeds. Numerous properties and businesses purchased by Humberto Garcia on behalf of the Gulf cartel have been identified and are in the process of being seized by the Mexican government. Juan Garcia Abrego was arrested and expelled from Mexico on January 15, 1996, and extradited to the United States. He was held without bond awaiting trial in Houston, Texas. Juan Garcia, the first foreign narcotics trafficker to be placed on the U.S. FBI's Most Wanted List, was held on a 1993 indictment on charges of cocaine trafficking, money laundering, and racketeering. The Garcia Abrego organization is responsible for the trafficking of marijuana and cocaine loads worth millions of dollars into the United States.

- In addition to these cases, Mexico has seized large bulk shipments of cash dollars, indicating a new alternative to more traditional methods of moving funds during the laundering process, such as wire transfers.
- In April 1995, U.S.$6 million in cash was discovered hidden inside a shipment of air conditioners.
- On October 9, 1995, troops of Mexico's 13th Military Zone command seized a Cessna 210 aircraft near Tepic, Nayari State. Inside, they found six suitcases containing U.S.$12 million, presumably the proceeds from drug sales of the Amado Carrillo Fuentes trafficking organization. The pilots were detained and turned over to Mexico's Federal Judicial Police in Tepic. The cash was turned in to the secretariat of national defense for eventual transfer to a general counternarcotics fund, in accordance with Mexican law.

Still, due to its proximity to the United States, as well as hemispheric narcotics production areas, Mexico remains a high priority for money-laundering activities and continues to be of considerable interest to U.S. law enforcement officials.

Moldova
(No priority.) As a signatory to the 1988 U.N. Convention, Moldova remains committed to conducting significant counternarcotics efforts. Although not a major producer or active in money-laundering operations, Moldova's status as a transshipment country has potential for exploitation by money launderers.

Monaco
(Low.) While not considered a major financial center, the Principality of Monaco may be vulnerable to money laundering. Casinos, which worldwide have proven to be used in money-laundering schemes, are a primary industry in Monaco, where money laundering is a crime and where suspicious transactions

must be reported. In June 1995, several high-level casino employees were arrested on corruption charges, as a result of an investigation ordered by Prince Ranier into money-laundering charges. In July 1995, an Israeli citizen was arrested when he attempted to deposit more than U.S.$5 million in a Moné-gasque bank. The money was seized, and the DEA is working with Monaco police to establish a drug nexus.

Morocco
(Medium.) The proceeds from narcotics exports from Morocco are easily repatriated. The government of Morocco makes no serious effort to trace drug or contraband money. There are in fact no laws against money laundering that would allow the Moroccan authorities to prosecute offenders effectively. Much of the revenue is invested in real estate, especially in northern Morocco, where drug money is an important source of income and has supported a construction boom. However, as increasing numbers of office and apartment buildings sit unoccupied, drug traffickers are reportedly casting about for new investment opportunities.

Namibia
(No priority.) Namibia is not a money-laundering center.

Nepal
(Low.) Nepal is not a money-laundering center.

Netherlands
(High.) The Netherlands is a major international financial center and, as such, offers opportunities for laundering funds generated from a variety of illicit or fraudulent activities, including narcotics trafficking. Money laundering is done through the banking system, money exchange houses, casinos, credit card companies, and insurance and securities firms.

Money laundered in the Netherlands is typically owned by major drug cartels and organized crime, often related to the sale of heroin, cocaine, or cannabis. The production and sale of cannabis products or designer drugs like MDMA (XTC or "ecstasy") is also giving rise to some money laundering. Some illicit currency transactions may well involve profits in dollars from illegal drug sales in Europe or elsewhere. There is no evidence yet of any U.S.-earned drug proceeds being laundered in the Netherlands, but it cannot be ruled out that the Dutch financial system could be used for this purpose.

Proceeds from non-drug crimes are also allegedly laundered in Amsterdam and other Dutch financial centers. A considerable portion of the illicit money laundered in the Netherlands is believed to have been generated through activities involving fraud.

The Dutch government has taken steps inspired by FATF initiatives, including imposing financial transaction-reporting requirements, against money laundering through the banking system, money-changing operations, casinos, and other operations involving large amounts of money. The laws apply to all criminal activity, not just to drug-related money laundering. Financial exchange houses came under regulation in January 1995. Dutch financial institutions normally deal with very significant amounts of U.S. currency derived from legitimate business operations.

The United States enjoys close cooperation with the Netherlands in fighting international crime, including money laundering. The Dutch (MOT) has close links with FinCEN and has submitted a draft cooperation agreement to FinCEN that is intended to increase that cooperation. The Dutch are also involved in efforts to expand cooperation between disclosure offices, particularly in Europe. In 1995, the Dutch took part in the Brussels and Paris meetings of the Egmont Group, which seeks to intensify cooperation between money-laundering disclosure offices in Europe and throughout the world. The Dutch have entered into bilateral agreements with many governments for the exchange of information on money laundering.

Adequate records can be made available officially to appropriate U.S. personnel through the MLAT with the Netherlands and the rogatory (letters of inquiry) commission. U.S. authorities cooperate closely with the Dutch Centrale Recherche Informatiedienst (CRI, the criminal intelligence service) and Internal Revenue Service Investigation Office.

The Netherlands has ratified the 1988 U.N. Convention and the 1990 Council of Europe Convention on Asset Forfeiture and Confiscation and is in compliance with FATF recommendations, as well as EU policy directives on money laundering. The Netherlands is active in FATF, which it chaired in 1994–95; CFATF, where it is a major donor; and the U.N. Commission on Narcotic Drugs, which it chaired in 1991. The Netherlands is a member of the major donors group of the UNDCP and an important contributor to EU counternarcotics efforts.

Dutch authorities cooperate closely with U.S. agencies on major money-laundering cases, which has resulted in significant seizures of assets in both countries. In 1995, in connection with its FATF-inspired anti-money-laundering activities, the Dutch government put bureaux de change, or money exchange offices, under the jurisdiction of Dutch banking legislation. Bureaux de change can now only operate with a license from the Netherlands central bank. As a result, the number of bureaux (which was considered too high for legitimate needs) has now decreased dramatically. Dutch money-laundering legislation targets transactions of more than 25,000 Dutch guilders or the foreign equivalent. Since February 1, 1994, all financial institutions, including bureaux de change, credit card companies, insurance and securities institutions, and casinos, must report transactions over 25,000 guilders or any transactions of less than that amount that appear suspicious.

Separate legislation, also in effect in 1994, mandates the checking of customer identity documents more frequently and for more types of transactions. Financial services can be provided only if the client's identity is established at the time or identity has been established previously. Identification is compulsory when a single transaction or a series of transactions exceed 25,000 guilders. Identification may also be demanded if the transaction is considered unusual for some reason. A refusal to show identification will make the transaction appear unusual or suspicious. Information about unusual transactions must be reported to the "unusual transactions disclosure office," a special office operating independently from law enforcement and judicial authorities but under the jurisdiction of the ministry of justice. Information is passed on for further action to the CRI only if the disclosure office believes that its own investigation has revealed a case of money laundering or another indictable offense. Information provided by a financial institution cannot be used against it, and there are protections for the financial institution against civil lawsuits as a result of the disclosure.

The Netherlands Justice Ministry recently reported on the activities of the money-laundering disclosure office from its inception in February 1994 to January 1995. During this period, it received 22,961 reports of "unusual financial transactions," mostly from commercial banks. Of this total, about 11.5 percent (2,638 transactions involving almost three billion guilders) were considered "financially suspect" and were investigated by the financial police ($1 equaled about 1.57 guilders when the report was made).

Twenty-nine cases yielded enough information to institute legal proceedings, but 900 of the unusual transaction reports were used in ongoing investigations. Most of the unusual financial transactions were made by Dutch, Belgian, and German citizens, although there had also been an increase in such transactions by individuals from the former Soviet Union. In 1994, the Amsterdam police operation Golden Calf resulted in the closure of a bureaux de change operated by Israeli citizens, the arrest of 25 people, and the seizure of 8 million guilders. Six people were eventually prosecuted and convicted.

The Netherlands government does not limit the amount of money that can be brought into or taken out of the country in bulk, but the changes in Dutch policies and laws related to money laundering have generally been accepted by legitimate financial institutions and businesses, which were initially opposed to them.

The Netherlands enforces the drug-related asset seizure and forfeiture laws that came into effect in 1994. Preliminary 1994 figures show that more than 800 asset seizure cases were in various stages of investigation and prosecution. Dutch prosecutors estimate that they will handle more than 3,000 cases a year for the next several years. Provisional 1994 figures show that assets seized amounted to more than 25 million guilders.

New Zealand

(Low priority.) New Zealand is not an important international banking center, nor is it considered a significant money-laundering center. There is no information that New Zealand or any senior official, as a matter of government policy, encourages, facilitates, or engages in money-laundering activities.

Nicaragua

(No priority.) Nicaragua is not an important regional financial center, nor is it considered a significant tax haven. What money is laundered appears to be narcotics related and could take place both in the banking and nonbanking financial system. The government does not, as a matter of policy, engage in money-laundering activities. The government was an active participant in the Summit of the Americas Money Laundering Ministerial Conference and signed the comprehensive ministerial communiqué that outlined a hemispheric action plan for combating money laundering.

Legislation enacted in 1996 will for the first time recognize money laundering (narcotics related or not) as a crime. The legislation requires banks and other financial institutions to report significant currency transactions. The government has yet to act to formally convene the banking commission established by the 1994 narcotics legislation to handle such matters. The 1994 legislation permits the seizure of any assets used in the commission of a narcotics-related crime and establishes how the money from the sale of such assets will be divided among the involved government ministries. To date, no goods have been seized under the new law.

Nigeria

(High.) Nigeria is not an important international financial center, but occupies the most important niche in the West African money-laundering situation, which is consistent with its high status as a drug transit country. Nigerians have become prominent as money launderers in the United States. Heroin proceeds are often used to purchase luxury automobiles and other commodities in the United States, Europe, and the Far East, which are then shipped to Nigeria and resold there or in neighboring countries. Proceeds from these sales are then deposited in banks in Nigeria or accounts that Nigerian traffickers hold abroad.

Nigeria announced a comprehensive national drug control strategy and passed a comprehensive Money Laundering Decree providing for the seizure and forfeiture of drug-related assets, such as the 16 Lagos car dealerships seized by the National Drug Law Enforcement Authority (NDLEA). The first prosecution under the decree is being prepared, and NDLEA expects a conviction.

The Money Laundering Decree requires the reporting of significant transactions to the central bank; regulates currency exchanges and gambling transactions; requires that records of significant or unusual transactions be shared with NDLEA, judicial, and customs officials; and provides for forfeiture of assets by individual and corporate violators.

An Advanced-Fee Fraud and Fraud Offenses Decree was also promulgated—a critical step, given the involvement of Nigerians around the world in advanced-fee fraud schemes. The decree not only outlaws such schemes and establishes penalties, it also criminalizes the laundering of funds obtained through such schemes.

This latter decree also contains a prohibition on transporting illicit funds, including electronic transfers of such proceeds. However, there are no laws governing the movement of hard currency into or out of Nigeria. The operative question is whether Nigeria will fully implement and enforce these new decrees.

Norway

(Low.) Norway is not a major world financial hub, tax haven, or offshore banking center. Money laundering is a criminal offense in Norway and is adequately investigated by a special police unit on economic crime. A law requiring that large money transactions be reported to this police unit was passed by parliament in December 1997. Laws on asset forfeiture and seizure are adequate and aggressively enforced, and drug-related money laundering is unusual.

Pakistan

(Medium-high.) Pakistan continues to be a significant producer of opium and refiner of heroin, as well as a transit route for Afghan opium, heroin, and cannabis. Pakistan, therefore, is a generator of illicit funds, which are laundered through the banking and nonbanking financial systems. Gold smuggling is also pervasive, as are invoicing schemes and other financial crimes. Illicit funds are also derived from contraband smuggling, but the ordinance that criminalized money laundering focuses exclusively on the proceeds of drug trafficking.

There have been improvements in the financial sector. Banks are now required to report suspicious transactions on request and to retain records over time. However, banks are not required to record significant cash transactions, nor is there a provision for sharing of banking data with third parties. There are no controls on the amount of money that can be brought into or taken out of Pakistan. Reports indicate that large sums of money from uncertain sources were poured into the country after the elimination of foreign exchange controls. There have been no recent arrests or prosecutions for money laundering.

Even the minimal reporting requirements are not imposed on nonbank institutions—an important omission given the purported vastness of the underground banking system (hundi) and the increasing importance of currency exchange houses.

Throughout this decade, Pakistani governments have been implementing policies designed to attract money from the black market into the legitimate economy. These measures have included liberalizing foreign currency and gold import restrictions, as well as issuing bearer bond schemes that have been literally advertised as an effective means to launder or conceal illegal proceeds. No identification is required to open a foreign-currency account, although it is required to open a Pakistani rupee account. Pakistanis can freely receive or transfer foreign currency, often at a price above the official rate. To facilitate this movement into banking mainstreams, since 1991 banks have not been required to report or maintain records on large currency transactions. Banks are also being privatized.

Economic reformers in Pakistan contend that this liberalization has been a positive step in strengthening Pakistan's legal economy. For example, the level of foreign exchange reserves has risen, including millions of U.S. dollars, since removal of foreign exchange controls. U.S. officials believe much of this money has been generated by illicit activities such as drug trafficking and tax evasion. There is less need for money launderers to use the hundi system if they have open access to the banking system.

The implementation of economic reform measures has boosted the involvement of currency exchange houses in money-laundering schemes, providing services that formerly were reserved for financial institutions, particularly in rural commercial centers. In one such location known to be used by drug traffickers, some money exchange houses have refused to handle transactions involving less than U.S.$1,000.

Panama

(High.) A Panamanian presidential decree in March 1995 established a permanent presidential money-laundering commission to oversee government money-laundering control efforts and formalized the national "drug czar" position. This commission is to ensure that all government agencies work cooperatively on money-laundering control and that key private sector groups do their part. Anti-money-laundering amendments, modifying Decree Law 41 of 1990 (Panama's criminal statute against money laundering), was passed in November 1995. It contains significant improvements to strengthen anti-money-laundering efforts, including know-your-client provisions, protection for bank officials who provide information on suspicious transacting and accounts, and prescribed punishment for violations of the code.

Under the law, suspicious transactions are reported to the banking commission and, in turn, to the financial analysis unit (FAU) that has been established in the Office of the Presidency. If the FAU concludes that money-laundering statutes have been violated, then the case is turned over to the Technical Judicial Police (PTJ) for criminal investigation and prosecution. The FAU collects and analyzes data on financial transactions in Panama to identify criminal activities. The FAU began start-up operations (e.g., setting up office, training, writing procedures) on July 3, 1995, and became more or less fully functional in the fall of 1996. The United States is supporting Panamanian efforts to form the FAU under the presidency and the PTJ's Financial Investigative Unit.

The new law is clearly a progressive step, but there are still concerns about other areas of vulnerability. For example, Panama continues to allow bearer-share corporations and the rules regarding records of beneficial ownership of corporations.

Money laundering in Panama is quite diversified. In addition to cash transactions through banks and contraband smuggling, money launderers are investing drug and other dollars in legitimate businesses, particularly construction. The Colon Free Zone (CFZ) is a money-laundering center in its own right. Presigned and prestamped blank invoices made out to fictitious companies are common, as are fraudulent invoices over- or underrepresenting goods shipped. Both methods are designed to cover money transfers.

In addition to cash deposits being placed in CFZ businesses, traffickers and smugglers are making large deposits of third-party checks drawn on U.S. banks, where cash deposits have accumulated through the use of various structuring techniques. Many of these checks have been transported from Colombia to Panama and are intended to give a legitimate cover to transactions. Also becoming quite popular are Mexican bank drafts, issued by banks in Mexico against their own dollar accounts in U.S. banks, a reflection in part of the substantial movement of drug cash in bulk in Mexico.

In May 1995, Panama undertook its first major money-laundering investigation in cooperation with the Canadian government. This investigation resulted in the arrests of four significant money launderers and the closure of five businesses in the CFZ. In October 1995, the Swiss police visited Panama to coordinate with the drug prosecutor's office in regard to two major money-laundering investigations. This resulted in the sharing of documentation covering major financial institutions that should assist both governments in prosecuting these money-laundering cases.

Based on federal warrants issued in the United States, the PTJ detained two of Panama's principal money launderers: Israel Mordok, an Israeli citizen, and Alberto Laila, a naturalized Panamanian. Mordok was extradited to the United States in October 1995 by Panamanian immigration officials, where he pleaded guilty to money-laundering charges. Due to his status as a Panamanian citizen, Laila was not extradited to the United States. Laila was arrested in the CFZ in October 1995 and initially held pending an extradition request, but was then released on U.S.$500,000 bond on December 28. Based on additional information from the United States, Laila was rearrested on February 16, 1996, on 11 counts of narcotics-related money laundering and will be prosecuted in a Panamanian court. Progress in the Laila case is seen as a barometer of the effectiveness of prosecuting Panamanian money launderers.

Panamanian law provides for seizure of narcotics-generated proceeds, but forfeiture of assets rarely happens. An exception to the rule was the approximately $40,000 in forfeited assets U.S. Customs shared with the Panamanian government subsequent to a narcotics trafficking case.

Paraguay

(Medium-high.) The high volume of foreign exchange transactions reported by the Paraguayan central bank in 1994 (U.S.$66 billion)—coupled with the large number of banks, a lack of regulation, a marked increase in cash businesses, and an absence of anti-money-laundering laws—raises serious questions about Paraguay's involvement in money laundering. There are no hard data on how much money is laundered in Paraguay or how much of the total comprising proceeds are from capital flight or contraband and narcotics smuggling. What is known is that Paraguay has an economy rated at U.S.$8 billion, with less than U.S.$1 billion in exports, but in 1994 returned more than U.S.$4 billion in excess currency to the United States, over 95 percent of that amount in $100 bills, substantially larger returns than the combined return of Brazil and Argentina's much larger economies. The informal opinion is that most money laundering is linked to the re-export sector (estimated variously at U.S.$4–14 billion, largely in contraband), followed by capital flight from Argentina and Brazil, with narcotics-related funds coming last.

Paraguay is considered an important tax haven, because there is no personal income tax or offshore banking center. Money laundering is not illegal and occurs in both the banking and nonbanking financial systems. There is no hard information on who controls money-laundering proceeds. While senior officials in the government condemn narcotics trafficking and laundering of drug proceeds, some officials are believed to encourage, facilitate, and engage in money-laundering activities based on re-export and capital flight proceeds. Notwithstanding the condemnation, Paraguay's government has not taken effective steps to criminalize this activity or to identify drug-related proceeds.

In 1994 Paraguay shipped U.S.$4.2 billion in excess U.S. currency to the United States, and the central bank recorded in excess of U.S.$35 billion in U.S. currency exchanges. It is unclear, however, whether these transactions were derived from illegal drug sales in the United States or their overall impact on the United States.

In 1994 Paraguay ratified a financial information exchange agreement (FIEA) with the United States. It has not adopted laws or regulations that ensure the availability of adequate records of narcotics investigations to appropriate U.S. personnel and those of other governments. Two draft bills currently under consideration by the U.S. Congress address this shortfall. The United States has yet to ask Paraguay for cooperation on an important case, and Paraguay has not refused to cooperate with foreign governments on any narcotics cases.

THE ART AND SCIENCE OF MONEY LAUNDERING

In 1995 the Paraguayan central bank issued regulations requiring banks and financial institutions to record transactions of more than U.S.$10,000: these records have to be kept for a period of five years. Paraguay permits but does not require financial institutions to report suspicious transactions; bankers and others are not fully protected by law with respect to their cooperation with law enforcement entities. The United States has yet to request cooperation from the government on financial crimes investigations under the FIEA.

Paraguay has not addressed the problem of international transportation of illegal-source currency and monetary instruments. There are no controls on the amount of currency that can be brought into or taken out of the country. While Law 1340 of 1988 provides a basic system for forfeiting narcotics-related assets, Paraguay has not enacted laws for sharing seized narcotics assets with other governments. Changes in current law are being contemplated to criminalize money laundering and update the existing national antidrug statute. However, in their current forms, neither bill provides for sharing seized assets. The chief obstacles to passage of such laws are an absence of political will, opposition from powerful economic interests, and congressional inefficiencies. Under current Law 1340, instruments of crime and intangible property derived from narcotrafficking (such as bank accounts) can be seized. Since money laundering is not a crime, legitimate businesses that launder drug money or other criminal proceeds are not subject to criminal sanctions. Also, it is an unresolved question whether a juridical person, such as a company, can be subject to criminal sanctions under Paraguayan jurisprudence. Since money laundering is not a crime, traffickers have not had an incentive to explore or test legal loopholes to help shield assets. Seized assets may only be forfeited once a suspect has been convicted. The law only provides for criminal forfeiture.

There has been no noticeable response to Paraguay's modest efforts to seize or forfeit assets. There have been no enforcement efforts to trace funds and seize bank accounts. Consequently, there has been no banking community cooperation in such efforts. As a matter of policy, the banking community has sought to preserve bank secrecy. There have been no money-laundering investigations or government cooperation with the United States on such investigations.

Peru

(Medium.) Peru is not a major global or regional financial center, tax haven, or offshore banking center. It is not considered a significant money-laundering center by U.S. authorities or foreign government officials. Money laundering related to narcotics proceeds occurs both in the banking system and the nonbank financial system of exchange dealers. Drug-related money laundering has hitherto largely represented funds repatriated by Peruvian cocaine-trafficking organizations for cocaine raw material purchasing, other expenses of trafficking activities (including corruption), and personal consumption by traffickers. These funds have included significant amounts of U.S. currency, usually derived from illegal cocaine sales in the United States by Colombian trafficking organizations, which then used that currency to purchase cocaine base from Peruvian trafficking organization suppliers. As Peru's economy continues to benefit from the most ambitious and successful stabilization program in the hemisphere, emerging market opportunities and investor confidence have encouraged increasing inflows of foreign capital. By no means do all such flows represent drug-related money laundering; investment of drug profits is becoming a more considerable factor than has previously been the case in Peru. As a matter of government policy, neither the government of Peru nor any senior official thereof encourages, facilitates, or engages in money-laundering activities. Peru became party to the 1988 U.N. Convention in 1992. It is not a member of FATF. Other than the provisions of the convention pertinent to mutual legal assistance, and international instruments dealing with such customary practices as interrogatories, Peru has no formal agreement with the United States on a general mechanism for exchanging records in connection with narcotics investigations and proceedings, and the United States has not requested negotiations with Peru on such an agreement.

In 1992, Peru and the United States concluded an agreement for exchange of information on cash transactions (the "Kerry amendment"). The Peruvian Superintendency of Banking and Insurance has published regulations to implement this agreement; the United States has made no formal requests for information under this agreement, and it is not known how well the regulations are implemented in practice. National police authorities responsible for narcotics investigation maintain good liaison relationships for the informal exchange of information with DEA on narcotics investigations, including money-laundering cases. Peru has a formal agreement with the United Kingdom for mutual assistance in narcotics enforcement, including asset sharing, and has provided information under that agreement. It has general agreements for counternarcotics cooperation with other countries, with some of which it also exchanges drug investigative information. No specific information is available on the extent of such exchanges, nor on how many countries may be involved.

Legislation adopted in 1992 made money laundering a criminal offense. Narcotics-related money laundering is an aggravated offense calling for additional penalties. Since the conclusion of the Kerry amendment agreement, banks and other financial institutions have been required under regulations adopted by the Superintendency of Banking and Insurance to know and record the identity of customers engaging in significant, large U.S. currency transactions, and to make this information available to the superintendency if required to respond to requests for information from the United States. Since economic stabilization and restoration of links with the international financial system began in 1990, U.S. currency has entered and left Peru free of exchange controls and circulates freely within Peru.

Financial institutions are not required to report suspicious transactions as such, and there is no indication that they do so. Peru has no due-diligence or banker-negligence laws making individuals responsible if institutions launder money. Peruvian police have cooperated when requested by DEA and by other government law enforcement authorities (e.g., in Canada, Germany, Italy, Spain, the United Kingdom) in investigations of narcotics cases, including financial crimes. Peruvian police capabilities to investigate large-scale, international, or sophisticated financial crimes are limited. There were a number of major asset seizures after the arrests of major drug traffickers (see below), but no major successful investigations of purely financial crimes during 1995 or the first six months of 1996. Some in the Peruvian banking community initially objected to the Kerry amendment agreement with the United States, but the objections have generally disappeared; most of the legitimate financial community, in such forums as U.S.-sponsored workshops or meetings with legal or enforcement experts on money laundering, now at least verbally endorse the desirability of measures to keep the financial system from becoming involved in laundering criminal drug-trafficking proceeds.

Under Peruvian criminal law, any property or assets used in the commission of a crime, or derived from the proceeds thereof, are subject to seizure and forfeiture. This applies to physical property, real and personal, and to financial property (including bank accounts), but a direct connection must normally be demonstrated between the property or assets in question and the antecedent narcotics or other criminal offense. Except in the instance of a prosecution brought by tax authorities because of a person's getting rich through trafficking in narcotics, there is no provision for civil forfeiture. Under a separate law, land on which coca is grown that has not been registered for coca cultivation with the Peruvian government (none has been since the 1970s) is subject to seizure and forfeiture.

Peru presently has no law for sharing seized narcotics assets with other governments; lack of such a law is one factor that continues to impede Peru's responding to a U.S. proposal to negotiate an asset-sharing agreement made in early 1992. The Ministry of Foreign Affairs indicated that such legislation would be considered by the government, but no such legislation is known to have been considered since. There are no significant disincentives to passing such a law; the main obstacle is the relative slowness of the Peruvian legislative system, and the lack of codification of laws covering narcotics offenses that makes any other relevant legislation difficult to frame. Assets seized in connection with narcotics offenses are delivered to the Ministry of the Interior's Office for Drug Control. This office is responsible for destruction of seized narcotics, custody of other assets pending completion of forfeiture proceedings, and distribution of forfeited assets to Peruvian government agencies for use in counternarcotics activities or other public purposes. The criminal code, as well as associated decrees referring to narcotics offenses, has been used as the basis for seizure and forfeiture by the Peruvian government of vehicles, aircraft, buildings, other property, and financial holdings of persons identified as drug traffickers. However, there is essentially no autonomous Peruvian institutional capability to identify, trace, or forfeit narcotics-related assets. Such activities customarily occur when assets are encountered in direct connection with commission of a narcotics offense; seizure arises from investigation or prosecution of an owner for such an offense by authorities in Peru or another country.

The arrest of three brothers and numerous associates of the Lopez Paredes trafficking organization in January 1995 was followed by seizure and forfeiture of several ranches, several thousand head of cattle (delivered to an agricultural school), numerous other pieces of real estate, bank accounts, and other property. When the major trafficker, Abelardo Cachique-Rivera, was arrested in Colombia and delivered to Peru for prosecution in June 1995, his interrogation disclosed many items of real property, bank accounts, and other assets, which were then seized. The law permitting seizure of land where unregistered coca cultivation takes place is seldom or never invoked and would be of little practical effect if it were, since most coca is actually grown by squatters on other owners' property or public lands.

The Philippines

(Medium.) The Philippines is not an important financial center, tax haven, or offshore banking center. A bill criminalizing money laundering has been introduced in the Philippine senate. Philippine bank secrecy laws make the amount and source of laundered money almost impossible to estimate.

Poland

(Medium.) Poland is not an important financial center, and money laundering is primarily related to tax evasion and other economic crimes, but the money laundered in Poland by local criminal organizations may include some proceeds from narcotics-related activities. Money laundering may occur in both the banking system and in exchange houses.

Current bank secrecy laws in Poland are very restrictive, normally allowing law enforcement or financial regulatory agencies access to customer accounts only if a crime has already been established and an indictment rendered. In this context, the banking community does cooperate with enforcement efforts to trace funds, but interprets the laws strictly. There are proposals to amend bank secrecy laws to bring them into line with the needs of law enforcement and regulatory authorities in combating financial crimes. The banking sector is neither opposing nor supporting the drafting of these amendments; however, no firm implementation dates have been set

There is no evidence that Polish financial institutions engage in any transactions involving narcotics-derived U.S. currency or otherwise significantly affecting the United States. There is no bilateral money-laundering agreement between Poland and the United States, although Polish officials consider the eventual negotiation and signing of such an agreement as vital. There are no laws ensuring U.S. access to narcotics investigations records. However, U.S. and Polish law enforcement agencies cooperate regularly and fully on narcotics investigations, with an open flow of information at the operational level.

Poland ratified the 1988 U.N. Convention in 1994. Poland is not a member of FATF; however, Poland's association agreement with the EU requires it to come into compliance with FATF recommendations. Money laundering is a criminal offense under legislation passed in 1994. The law is not limited to drug-related money laundering. Banks are required to know and record the identity of customers engaging in currency transactions over 20,000 zloty (PLN), approximately U.S.$8,000. They are required to report suspicious transactions and maintain these and all financial records for at least five years. Suspicious transactions are reported to the local prosecutor's office. However, discretion lies with the individual bank employee handling a transaction (sometimes simply a window cashier) as to whether the transaction is suspicious or not. Bankers are not protected by law with respect to their cooperation with law enforcement authorities. Under Polish banking regulations, individual bankers are "professionally" responsible if their institutions launder money and are subject to civil liability. The banking sector is reluctant to loosen bank secrecy laws. However, regulators believe that most banks recognize that effective money-laundering controls are in their own long-term interest.

Poland does not have specific laws dealing with the international transportation of illegal-source currency and monetary instruments. Such transactions are by nature limited by Polish foreign-exchange control laws, which require that all foreign transfers of currency and monetary instruments be documented by source and destination. However, Polish authorities admit that such "legal" documentation can be easily arranged for a price, regardless of the reality of the transaction. The foreign transfer of Polish currency is prohibited. International transportation of foreign currency obtained from exchange houses is not permitted. However, there are no requirements for the recording of the identity of individuals changing money at exchange houses. Exchange houses are the only legal nonbanking financial institutions in Poland.

The Polish National Police conducted 11 investigations in 1995 under the new money-laundering law, which became effective December 31, 1994. Two of these cases have been passed on to prosecutors, together involving the laundering of at least 40 million PLN (U.S.$16 million). Eight money-laundering arrests were made; however, to date, there have been no criminal convictions for money laundering. Although it is insufficiently broad, the 1994 money-laundering law provides for the seizure and forfeiture of crime-related assets. Seizure of assets in money-laundering cases was not permitted before 1995, and there is no legislation in force that specifically applies to narcotics-related money laundering.

There is no system in place specifically designed to identify, trace, seize, freeze, or forfeit assets resulting from criminal activity, drug related or otherwise. Law enforcement agencies and regulators are limited to existing inadequate financial crime laws in their efforts in this area. Poland has not enacted laws for sharing seized narcotics assets with other governments. Only financial instruments or other assets that can in some way be linked to an actual crime are subject to seizure or forfeiture. If it is proven to have been used in the commission of a crime, a legitimate business can be seized; if such is not proven, the business or other asset may only be seized as settlement against a court-imposed fine. In particular, joint ownership or transfer of ownership to a family member or third party can make the attachment of assets difficult for Polish authorities.

The government does have the authority to forfeit seized assets. Both civil and criminal asset seizure is possible under Polish law, but they are mutually exclusive; once a court decides that either the criminal or civil code applies to a given case, the other code cannot be invoked. The Polish Ministry of Justice and others are preparing draft legislation to bring Poland into compliance with the 1990 Strasbourg Convention on money laundering and asset forfeiture, as specifically required by Poland's association agreement with the EU. At present the Polish government has neither adequate police powers nor resources to trace and seize assets effectively. Polish authorities seized U.S.$250,000 in cash and U.S.$10,000 worth of property and equipment related to money laundering in late 1995. Disposition of these assets is still awaiting a ruling from the courts with jurisdiction in the cases.

Portugal

(Low-medium.) The Portuguese Financial Unit has several ongoing money-laundering investigations. The Portuguese antinarcotics effort has been assisted with training provided by U.S. agencies recently, as well as being strengthened by money-laundering and financial laws enacted in 1994. However, the 1908 Extradition Treaty between the United States and Portugal is out of date; it does not cover such "modern" offenses as money laundering and financial crimes.

Romania

(Low.) Romania has declared its intent to extend its international cooperation in combating illegal drugs into the money-laundering arena, and there is some indication that new laws are being prepared regarding drug trafficking, control of narcotics precursors, and money laundering. Many draft laws remain mired in the parliamentary process. Romanian concern about the presence of Russian and Italian mafiosi, Chinese organized crime groups, and South American drug cartels has sparked an interest in moving forward on the new laws. The banking system is underdeveloped and is considered unattractive for potential money laundering.

Russia

(High.) As evidence continues to mount that organized crime groups are controlling large sectors of the economy, U.S. concerns about the inadequate management of Russia's financial system with respect to money laundering and other financial crimes has prompted raising the priority for Russia to high, putting Russia among those nations for which the United States believes immediate remedial action is necessary.

Criminal and fraudulent activities in the Russian banking sector (and the perception of such activities) have serious implications for the safety and soundness of the banking system and consumer confidence in the commercial banks as an integral institutional component of a market economy. There has been substantial speculation about the control of Russian banks, with one source estimating that 25 percent of Moscow's commercial banks are controlled by organized crime. For one thing, the Russian *mafiya* allegedly uses bank records to obtain information about companies for extortion purposes. Reports that money laundering, including funds derived from illegal narcotics transactions, raise questions of a serious problem in commercial banks in Russia. Although most such activity in

Russia is thought to involve the laundering of funds from illegal activities not related to narcotics, reports abound of Russian banks' laundering of narcotics money for organized crime groups outside Russia (e.g., Cali cartel, Sicilian Mafia). The central bank of Russia, working with the multilateral FATF, is introducing reporting and other requirements to combat money laundering.

Moscow is considered an important financial center in the former Soviet Union, but it is not considered an important tax haven. Money laundering allegedly occurs in banks, exchange houses, insurance companies, and real estate firms. The use of false contracts for import and export as a means of hiding revenue offshore has diminished somewhat recently with better customs and banking regulations over external trade and increasing financial stabilization in Russia. In addition, in 1995 the central bank revoked the licenses of 315 badly managed banks—12 percent of the banking industry—and restricted operations for another 423. This is in contrast to the revocation of only 85 licenses in the preceding four years.

San Marino

(Low.) There have been two events of note in San Marino. First, a Bank of Italy study disclosed that deposits in San Marino, which has a strong tradition of bank secrecy, were three times higher than its GNP and that per capita bank deposits were 10 times higher than in Italy. Second, San Marino, which is subject to Italian banking regulations, announced in late 1995 that its officials had signed the Council of Europe Convention, which commits the government to adopt legislation on money laundering, therefore permitting the courts to order disclosure of banking and commercial records, including documents requested by foreign governments for criminal investigation purposes.

Senegal

(No priority.) There has been speculation that narcotics money has been invested in some of Senegal's coastal tourist resorts, but this has not been corroborated. There have been no other indications that Senegal, which has ratified the 1988 U.N. Convention, is experiencing a money-laundering problem.

Seychelles

(Low.) There is currently no evidence that substantial money laundering is underway, but the Seychelles attracted substantial international attention and criticism by adopting measures that have an inherent potential for attracting illegal proceeds. The Economic Development Act, officially adopted in December 1995, offers large-scale investors who invest in Seychelles a no-questions-asked opportunity to deposit proceeds from any source, as well as protection against international requests for extradition and asset seizures.

The language of the act, ostensibly designed to attract large foreign investments, strongly suggests that its intention is to draw tainted money. Under the act, the Seychelles can grant someone investing more than $10 million "immunity from prosecution for all criminal proceedings whatsoever." The government also has authority to grant "immunity from compulsory acquisition or sequestration of the assets belonging to an investor." The United States and other nations, notably the United Kingdom and France, have made it known that they have great concern with this legislation.

The Seychelles has also announced plans to set up an offshore banking system, with secret, numbered accounts and a securities (stock market) system. The government maintains that it is not seeking to encourage money laundering. However, the Economic Development Act was passed by the 26-nation FATF on January 30, 1996, which asked nations to consider unusual transactions involving the Seychelles as potentially suspicious.

Singapore

(High.) Singapore is one of Asia's most important financial centers and one of the world's fastest growing foreign-exchange markets. U.S. and Singaporean officials disagree on the extent of money laundering through Singapore's banking system. Information sharing, which may reveal more of the level at which criminals are operating, was enhanced in 1996 on a designation agreement that will enable U.S. authorities to participate in the processes enabled by the Singaporean anti-money-laundering laws.

Until the 1994 anti-money-laundering law allowed the sharing of banking data in accord with bilateral agreements, information sharing in Singapore had been virtually precluded under bank secrecy laws, with only rare exceptions. U.S. officials believe that significant laundering occurred in both the banking and nonbanking financial systems of exchange houses.

Penalties for money laundering are onerous, including seizure of the account. Narcotics-associated money laundering is a criminal offense, in conformity with the 1988 U.N. Convention. Bankers can be held personally liable in money-laundering cases. Under the Drug Trafficking (confiscation of benefits) Act of 1992, banks must report suspicious transactions. Banks must positively identify customers engaging in large currency transactions. There are no controls or reporting requirements on amounts of currency that can be brought into or taken out of Singapore. Banks maintain adequate records to respond quickly to government inquiries in narcotics-related cases. Although reporting requirements placed on the legitimate banking sector are quite extensive, it is not yet clear how effectively the new legislation will restrict money-laundering activities in the less-regulated system of exchange houses.

Singapore has internal procedures for identifying, tracing, freezing, seizing, and forfeiting narcotics-related assets. The

United States has worked closely with Singaporean counterparts in identifying several major accounts that the Singapore government froze in August 1994. Conveyances, bank accounts, and businesses can be seized under the law, and the proceeds go to the government. The United States knows of no loopholes that shield assets, although the law does protect the assets of innocent third parties. Singapore's narcotics officers are responsible for tracing and seizing assets, with the assistance of the Commercial Affairs Division of the Ministry of Finance. Limited information sharing in money-laundering cases is available under the 1992 legislation; however, enabling legislation requires that the government conclude an MOU or MLAT with foreign governments to gain access to such information. Singapore is not a signatory to the 1988 U.N. Convention, but it is a member of FATF.

Slovakia
(Medium.) Slovakia's banking sector remains primarily under state control, with only a handful of private banks currently operating in the country. Law enforcement officials believe (although they have no firm evidence on which to base this conclusion) that Slovakian banks, both state run and private, are involved in money laundering. Anecdotal information suggests that criminal organizations have increasing influence and engage in illicit financial activity. Unfortunately, the police do not have the experience or the resources to even begin to look at this problem. Therefore, it is impossible to identify precisely the type of money laundering being carried out or to state categorically that it is related to narcotics trafficking.

There is no formal information-sharing mechanism between U.S. and Slovak law enforcement entities. There do exist, however, good informal contacts through which requests for information related to specific cases are passed. It is not known if Slovakia has similar arrangements with any other countries.

Money laundering is incorporated as a criminal offense in the Slovak penal code; however, banks are under no requirement to report large cash transactions to a central authority. In addition, the authorities are simply not equipped to begin to focus attention on this problem.

South Africa

(Low-medium.) South Africa is the major financial center in Southern Africa and has great potential as a money-laundering base. Money-laundering legislation written in 1995 came before South African parliament in early 1996 and was passeed in November of the same year. All the same, assets used by persons convicted of narcotics-related crimes may be seized under the 1992 Drug Control Act and turned over to the state treasury.

The U.S. Department of Treasury (including the Office of Asset Forfeiture, ATF, Customs, IRS, and Secret Service) conducted a highly successful money-laundering and asset forfeiture conference in September 1995. South African customs, however, is a revenue-collecting agency in the middle of a major reorganization, and there are bureaucratic obstacles that have to be surmounted before customs can take over narcotics interdiction at ports of entry.

Spain

(Medium-high.) Spain is increasingly aware of its potential as a significant money-laundering center. Spanish financial institutions are being used by traffickers to launder illicit proceeds. The banks and financial institutions of neighboring Gibraltar and Andorra are similarly used. However, Spanish financial institutions are increasingly sensitive to the modus operandi and signature of money-laundering activities, which has led these institutions to be more cooperative in combating money-laundering activities.

Money laundering in Spain is probably mostly related to narcotics proceeds, and money laundering occurs primarily in the financial system, though there is increasing evidence that money is laundered through the acquisition and sale of real estate. Illicit activities are directly related to the sale or distribution of heroin, cocaine, and marijuana; thus, money-laundering activities in Spain often originate with large Latin American drug cartels.

According to Spanish national law enforcement reports, an undetermined, yet significant, amount of illicit proceeds are estimated to arrive in the United States from Spanish financial institutions each year. There is an agreement between the United States and Spain on the exchange of records in connection with narcotics investigations and proceeds from these criminal activities; that is, Spain has adopted laws and regulations that ensure the availability of records of narcotics investigations to appropriate U.S. personnel and those of other governments.

Spain has signed and ratified the 1988 U.N. Convention. Spain is a member of FATF and is the originator and founder of the "Madrid group," a coalition of eight Western European countries' national directors and heads of antidrug agencies. The group exchanges information and intelligence on all aspects of criminal narcotics activity.

Money laundering became a criminal offense in Spain in December 1992, punishable by imprisonment or fine. December 1993 legislation expanded money-laundering activities to include terrorism and organized crime.

Banks and other financial institutions are required to report the identity of customers engaging in significant large currency transactions. Banks and other financial institutions are required to maintain sufficient records to reconstruct significant transactions through financial institutions. This enables banks to respond quickly to information requests from appropriate government authorities in narcotics-related inquiries. The Bank of Spain is the central, long-term depository of financial records.

Branch offices of all banks operating in Spain maintain short-term records, as well as providing them to the central bank daily. Bankers and others are protected by law with respect to their cooperation with law enforcement entities.

Spain is in full compliance with the 1988 U.N. Convention and its MLAT with the United States. Spain has cooperated fully with U.S. law enforcement agencies and those of other governments investigating financial crimes related to narcotics trafficking and money laundering. It has also addressed the problem of international transportation of illegal-source currency and monetary instruments. There are controls on the amount of currency that can be brought into or out of Spain, but the courts continue to apply lenient sentences when these controls are violated.

Spain continues to enforce the due-diligence and banker-negligence laws in the money-laundering legislation approved in December 1993. The money-laundering controls are also applied to nonbanking financial institutions, such as casas de cambio. There has been no notable decline in deposits attributable to changes in money-laundering laws, but there have been arrests, seizures, forfeitures, and prosecutions for money laundering. The ongoing "charlines" case, involving a Galician crime organization in northwestern Spain, is the most significant recent case. In 1995 Spain adopted broader laws permitting the use of controlled shipments, the forfeiture of drug traffickers' assets, and the use of undercover agents to infiltrate narcotics rings to gain evidence. The 1995 legislation also permits controlled money pickups to facilitate money-laundering investigations. Financial instruments, real estate, or personal property—particularly boats, automobiles, and even shops or bars—may be seized or frozen.

Spain has made progress, albeit slowly, to work with other governments to identify, trace, and freeze narcotics assets. With the recent passage of legislation and revisions to the penal code, Spain is likely to coordinate more closely in the future with foreign governments in the areas of identifying, tracing, and freezing assets resulting from drug trafficking. Under recently passed legislation, the government of Spain may share in asset forfeitures. National laws do not yet permit sharing of forfeited assets with other countries. This new legislation is intended to close legal loopholes that would otherwise allow traffickers and others to shield assets. Legislation allows for criminal forfeiture of assets seized in narcotics-related activities.

The Spanish national police narcotics division and the Guardia Civil are all entitled to investigate criminal offenses related to drug money laundering. Under recently approved legislation, Spanish national law enforcement agencies are empowered to both seize and enforce forfeiture proceedings. The dollar amount of assets seized in narcotics operations in 1994 by Spanish law enforcement authorities was roughly U.S.$10.5 million, a 20-fold increase over the previous year. This increase is due primarily to passage of money-laundering legislation and the 60-ton increase in confiscated hashish in 1994. The government of Spain is engaged in bilateral or multilateral negotiations with other governments to harmonize efforts regarding asset tracing and seizure.

Sri Lanka

(Low.) Sri Lanka is not considered a major money-laundering center, nor is it considered a tax haven, offshore banking center, or an important financial center in the region. The country does not facilitate or encourage money laundering as a matter of government policy. Current legislation specifically excludes transactions relating to narcotics trafficking under its Bank Secrecy Act. Draft legislation amending the dangerous drugs ordinance to include specific provisions against money laundering, prepared by the National Dangerous Drugs Control Board (NDDCB), has not been presented to parliament. Sri Lanka is a signatory to the 1988 U.N. Convention.

Sudan
(No priority.) Sudan is not a drug money-laundering center.

Suriname
(Low.) The primarily Dutch-owned banks are sensitive to money-laundering methodology, and money laundering by outside drug interests does not appear to be taking place. There are no structures in the country that would lend themselves to international drug money laundering. However, laundering of money through real estate acquisitions and investments by local traffickers is of continuing concern. The government has no programs in place to identify or inhibit that illicit activity, but the Summit of the Americas Money Laundering Conference and communiqué are heightening the awareness of Suriname's officials to the dangers of money laundering.

Sweden
(Low.) Sweden is not an important money-laundering center, but the government has ratified the 1988 U.N. Convention and criminalized money laundering. In compliance with the 1988 U.N. Convention and FATF recommendations, Sweden requires banks and other financial institutions to record and report the identity of customers engaging in significant or suspicious transactions. Sweden also has asset forfeiture and seizure laws relative to drug-trafficking offenses. The police have established a National Financial Intelligence Service Unit to enforce these laws.

Switzerland
(High.) Switzerland is one of the world's leading financial centers, and its very sophisticated banking system, like those of other key financial centers, remains vulnerable to exploitation by money launderers—and it often is. Money laundered in Switzerland involves proceeds from the sale of the three major drugs (cocaine, heroin, and marijuana) but also includes pro-

ceeds from other serious crimes. Switzerland serves as a transit point for money, licit and illicit, as well as a conversion point.

The major traffickers themselves are usually not present in Switzerland during these transactions, which are conducted by middlemen, including professional money launderers. Switzerland is in fact more important as a tax haven than as a money-laundering site, since Swiss law does not allow legal assistance if tax evasion is the only alleged crime. Money laundering occurs through banks and nonbanking financial institutions. Approximately U.S.$425 million has been frozen in Swiss banking institutions since 1990 and was identified primarily through narcotics investigations by the DEA.

U.S. and Swiss authorities have cooperated in many important cases. Whereas U.S. authorities are required under the Swiss-U.S. MLAT to work through Swiss central government authorities, most actual enforcement in Switzerland takes place at the cantonal level. Switzerland routinely coordinates and exchanges information on money-laundering cases with other countries, primarily the United States.

Switzerland has signed the 1988 U.N. Convention, and the Swiss government will seek ratification in 1997. Switzerland is a member of FATF and has moved to effectively implement FATF recommendations.

The Swiss penal code has explicitly recognized money laundering as a criminal offense since August 1990. The failure by banks or agents to exercise due diligence in identifying the beneficial owner of assets entrusted to their care also carries criminal sanctions. The requirement that trustees disclose the names of benefiting owners effectively lifted the veil of bank secrecy from the fabled Swiss numbered bank account. This first package of measures permitted Switzerland to participate actively in international cooperation, but did not deter money laundering to the degree desired. Consequently, the Swiss federal cabinet and parliament adopted a second package of measures that came into force on August 1, 1994. These measures criminalize membership in or support of a criminal organization. The change in the law facilitates confiscation of illicitly acquired assets without having to establish an exact linkage between a given asset and a specific crime. In addition, the revised penal code allows bank employees to report suspicious transactions without fear of violating the bank secrecy regulations.

In 1994, the Swiss federal government presented a third package of measures that would extend the money-laundering legislation to nonbanking financial institutions and establish an obligation to report suspicious transactions. Nonbanking financial institutions, such as bureaux de change, are not affected by the due-diligence convention or by the circular letter from the Swiss federal banking commission, since the commission has no authority over them. They are, however, subject to the penal code, notably the code's requirement for due diligence in identifying the beneficial owner of assets and its prohibition against money laundering.

In 1995, a federal administrative body was created to lead the fight against organized crime. This office coordinates operations between the cantons, collects and distributes information on organized crime, and develops contacts with similar bodies abroad. In order to implement FATF recommendations, the Swiss banking commission prepared a circular letter that took effect in 1992. Swiss banks are already self-regulated on the issue of customer identification through the due-diligence convention of 1987. This convention requires Swiss bankers to identify the benefiting owner of accounts and provides sanctions against banks that fail to live up to the convention. The convention was renewed in 1992 and strengthened to conform with FATF regulations and the circular letter. Banks are required to maintain records of currency transactions of SFR (Swiss francs) 100,000 or more; they are not required to report this data to a central authority. The banking commission, in consultation with the banks, plans to lower this threshold to SFR 25,000.

Switzerland, like several other financial centers, has never restricted international capital movements, relying instead on internal controls. Concern that a lack of restrictions on cross-border currency movements could abet money laundering has spurred the Swiss government to sponsor legislation designed to curb any such abuses.

In November 1995, the Colombian national Sheila Miriam Arana de Nasser confessed in a Miami court to money laundering. Using this confession, U.S. and Swiss authorities anticipate dividing U.S.$160 million in blocked Swiss bank accounts. At present, Swiss officials are cooperating with U.S. and Mexican officials in the sensitive investigation of money-laundering charges involving members of the Salinas Gortarí family; more than U.S.$100 million is frozen in Swiss-controlled bank accounts in this case.

Switzerland ratified the Council of Europe Convention on Asset Forfeiture and Confiscation. Notably, Swiss forfeiture law is not limited to narcotics trafficking cases, but instead focuses on criminal activity in general. The new law that came into force on August 1, 1994, allows confiscation of assets equivalent in value to the wealth derived from criminal activity. Judges have authority to estimate the amount of wealth that a criminal has earned illegally. The court can then order confiscation of assets up to the established amount of criminal wealth, without having to prove that these assets derive from crime. If assets are forfeited, the proceeds go into the general budget of the canton in which the legal action took place. The measure introduced in August 1994 also shifts the burden of the proof vis-à-vis the acquisition of wealth to the accused.

Syria

(Low.) Syria is considered neither an important regional financial center nor a significant drug-money-laundering center. The absence of private banks, combined with harsh penalties for illegal currency dealings, limits money laundering, which, although possible, is much easier to carry out in neighboring Lebanon.

Taiwan

(Medium.) Experts say money laundering in Taiwan is not solely connected to narcotics trafficking, but is also related to activities such as illegal manufacturing and insider trading on the securities market. Money laundering in Taiwan has been a largely underground phenomenon, with jewelry stores, leasing companies, and pawnshops serving as major capital movement channels.

Taiwan is continuing an active counternarcotics effort that includes harsh sentences for narcotics trafficking—including capital punishment under existing laws—as well as social rehabilitation programs. New legislation, designed to augment existing counternarcotics laws and bring Taiwan into conformity with the 1988 U.N. Convention as well as the recommendations of the financial and chemical action task forces relating to money laundering and precursor chemical controls, is under legislative consideration.

Tajikistan

(No priority.) Tajikistan is not a money-laundering center.

Tanzania

(No priority.) Certain foreign investments on the Tanzania mainland and on the island of Zanzibar are alleged to be linked with money-laundering activities, though hard evidence is lacking. Little information is available concerning money laundering in Tanzania. The lack of experience and training among bank officials and local law enforcement authorities is reflected in their lack of information.

Thailand

(High.) Thailand is an important and growing regional center for financial activities whose importance in the worlds of both licit and illicit capital movement has not been matched to date by commensurate measures to prevent money laundering and other financial crimes. Thailand's efficient network of banks and financial institutions is used by drug traffickers to move and hide their proceeds throughout Asia. Thus Thailand remains one of the key money-laundering concerns in Asia. Although these problems remain, two succeeding governments pushed to introduce money-laundering legislation, a move that has official, business, and public support. These laws were enacted in the spring 1996 parliamentary session.

Rapid economic growth, real estate investment, and an active stock market coupled with a major presence of international financial institutions make Thailand an attractive investment site. Thai investment in the region, especially in the economies of Cambodia, Laos, Vietnam, and Burma, is a consequence of comparatively rapid economic growth and burgeoning investment capital and the fact that its banking and financial service sectors are far more developed than those of neighboring countries. An offshore banking facility in Bangkok, specifically designed to meet the needs of outside investors in these neighboring countries, was created in 1992.

Besides the official financial system, an extensive informal and less regulated financial system exists. This—coupled with the presence of large amounts of money from the illicit drug trafficking, smuggling of commodities and arms, and from gambling, prostitution, counterfeiting, and other extralegal practices—has created a situation where, in the opinion of most international experts, money laundering is inevitable and relatively widespread. A committee set up under the authority of the prime minister's office completed a draft of money legislation in the spring of 1995. This legislation was not introduced in parliament due to the dissolution of the previous government in May. Following the July elections, resulting in the formation of a new coalition government, the draft legislation was again under consideration by the government.

Since there is an absence of appropriate money-laundering legislation and current bank secrecy practices make it nearly impossible for the Royal Thai government itself to obtain the financial information required for narcotics-related financial investigations, little action has been taken to target the financial underpinnings of illegal activities, including drug trafficking and other forms of smuggling. The issue is not the government's willingness to share information so much as the inability under the present legal situation to obtain such information. Thailand has participated in meetings of the FATF and consulted with the governments of the United States, Great Britain, and Australia and with the United Nations to gain information about money-laundering laws and control systems. Thailand's current efforts to enact money-laundering legislation are, in part, a response to the urgings of FATF and other foreign countries, including the Dublin Group.

Passage of appropriate money-laundering legislation is the last hurdle Thailand needs to cross to permit it to accede to the 1988 U.N. Convention.

Pending the passage of the money-laundering legislation, the only drug-related law governing assets is the 1991 Thai Asset Seizure Law. Proposed money-laundering legislation currently being reviewed by the government would initially criminalize only drug-related money laundering. Thai officials and members of the drafting committee have indicated that this initial restriction, believed necessary to get the legislation passed into law, should in the future be relaxed to cover money laundering of funds from any illicit source. The legislation-drafting committee has studied a number of different legal models including U.N. and OAS model regulations and has built bank-reporting requirements into the law, as well as provisions protecting bankers from the consequences of their compliance with the reporting requirements. One area of U.S. concern is the lack of specific language in the draft legislation covering the sharing of information internationally.

An asset-seizure law was passed in 1991 and implemented in 1992. Until this year progress appeared slow in gaining convictions under the law. In September 1995, Thai authorities completed the first successful prosecutions under the asset seizure and conspiracy statutes. According to Thai officials, the newness of the legislation and the government's desire to present very solid cases accounted for the apparent slowness of implementation leading to these initial successes. It is hoped in the future that prosecutions and convictions will proceed more rapidly.

The Property Examination Committee of the Office of the Narcotics Control Board (ONCB) is the body having primary responsibility for action under the asset seizure law. Most recently, a total of 138 cases involving more than U.S.$9 million in assets have been brought under the asset seizure law. Property Examination Committee officials have received good cooperation from banks and other financial institutions in instances where seizure orders have been issued, but, absent legislation requiring them to do so, banks will not necessarily provide information to law enforcement officials to assist in investigations.

Under the asset seizure and conspiracy laws, enforcement officials are not permitted to open investigations or bring charges relating to assets connected to drug-related crimes committed before the implementation date of the act. As time passes, this limitation will diminish in importance.

Trinidad and Tobago

(Low-medium.) Money laundering may take place in banks, credit unions, stock brokerages, and insurance companies, but no cases have established the extent of money laundering. Information is shared informally and through official channels such as CFATF. The government is currently negotiating a mutual legal assistance treaty with the United States. It has ratified the 1988 U.N. Convention. Money laundering is a criminal offense, not limited to drug trafficking. Banks voluntarily report transactions involving sums exceeding approximately U.S.$8,000 in cash. Banking records must be maintained for 14 years, and the law requires banks to report suspicious transactions. Bankers and others reporting a suspicious transaction are protected by law from prosecution. Travelers entering and departing Trinidad and Tobago must declare currency of U.S.$5,000 or more to customs; cash above U.S.$10,000 in value may be seized by customs, with judicial approval, pending determination of its legitimate source.

Money-laundering guidelines, set by the central bank, apply only to banks. However, employees of credit unions or exchange houses are subject to money-laundering penalties. There have not been any arrests or prosecutions for money laundering.

Turkey

(High.) Turkey is one of the three nations whose priority was raised to high in 1996, indicating the belief by the U.S. government that immediate remedial action is necessary to counter money-laundering practices. This assessment also takes into account deep concerns about the inadequacies of current law and uncertainties about the effectiveness of new laws that have been promised.

The increased priority assigned to Turkey is rooted partly in concerns that money laundering there is not limited to drug proceeds but includes proceeds from other criminal activity. Although there is no consensus as to whether actual volumes of transactions have increased, there is no question about the need for Turkey to demonstrate the political will to make these changes before the problem worsens. Turkey remains one of the few members of FATF that has not adopted legislation to meet international standards. Money laundering may not be the most critical problem confronting the Turkish government, but it deserves a higher political priority than it has received in the past.

Given the prominence of Turkish drug-trafficking organizations in the European drug market, Turkey is also considered to be a high priority for money laundering because of the likelihood that some drug profits are returned to Turkey for investment in legitimate businesses.

Draft legislation currently under consideration is not perfect, but its adoption would be a major step toward meeting Turkey's obligations under the 1988 U.N. Convention. As currently drafted, the proposed law would criminalize money laundering involving the proceeds of all crimes, not just drug trafficking, and include the proceeds of contraband smuggling as well as funding of terrorist organizations. Among the bill's important impacts, a new "financial crimes research and investigation administration" would have sole responsibility for controlling money laundering. The bill would strengthen existing asset seizure laws to bring them into line with the 1988 U.N. Convention.

Money laundering is not now prohibited or controlled. Turkey has taken other steps that are consistent with global money-laundering countermeasures. The central bank requires banks every month to report transactions above three billion Turkish lira (U.S.$50,000), together with customer identification. This information goes to the Treasury and Finance Ministry. The banking law requires banks and financial institutions to maintain all documents—originals if possible—related to their operations. The Turkish commercial code requires all entities to keep their records for 10 years.

Turkmenistan

(No priority.) The growing number of casinos and foreign-run luxury hotels has raised concern among some observers about Turkmenistan's vulnerability to becoming a haven for money-laundering activities associated with the narcotics trade. Turkmenistan is not a signatory to the 1988 U.N. Convention, but its government is considering accession at this time.

Uganda
(No priority.) Kampala, the capital, is experiencing a dramatic influx of Western currency, primarily from nongovernment organizations and donor nations. Ugandan authorities assume that some of the funds transferred into Uganda may also be from illicit sources, but there is no indication of a large volume of illicit money, and authorities concede that they themselves lack the expertise to conduct effective investigations.

Ukraine
(Low.) Capital flight presents a more serious problem in Ukraine than money laundering. Ukraine is not a financial center in its own right: the Ukrainian banking sector remains below Western standards. Some laundering is undertaken by Russian organized crime in the Crimea, which is a haven for the criminals and Russian banks, but Ukrainian criminal groups are assumed to transfer much of their profits to Europe. Legislation was passed in 1995 that creates legal mechanisms to prevent capital flight and provides for asset seizure and forfeiture of money and property derived from illegal activities. Government authorities take the problems of capital flight and money laundering very seriously and have pushed parliament to pass laws to restrict such activities.

United Arab Emirates
(Medium-high.) Although not on the same scale as East Asian banking centers, the open and accessible banking system of the United Arab Emirates (UAE) makes this political entity an important regional financial center. Currently, the UAE does not have laws to restrict or prevent money laun-

dering, nor does it have disclosure laws, so no information is available on the sources of assets held by UAE banks. Given the UAE's proximity to regional drug-producing countries, however, it is likely that trafficking organizations use UAE banks to launder their narcotics proceeds.

The UAE is not considered an important tax haven or off-shore banking center. Money laundering is currently not illegal in the UAE. Both the banking system and the nonbanking financial system (primarily the hawala system used widely throughout South Asia) are open and flourishing. Currently, no information is available on the extent to which UAE banks are used for laundering or on the organizations involved in money laundering. The UAE has been working on legislation to control money laundering for the past few years and reportedly has draft legislation in place. The UAE does not have foreign currency controls, and U.S. dollars, like other foreign currencies, are freely exchanged. The UAE does not have laws allowing for asset forfeiture and seizure.

United Kingdom

(High.) U.K. banks and other financial institutions share the vulnerability to money laundering experienced by the world's major banking centers. Narcotics proceeds are converted in the United Kingdom but also transit the country. The Channel Islands and the Isle of Man have offshore banking facilities that are also believed to attract drug funds and have adopted money-laundering countermeasures.

The United Kingdom has comprehensive legislation aimed at preventing money laundering. The government moves swiftly to plug loopholes. Between January 1987 and December 1994, there were 102 prosecutions for money laundering. U.S. agencies work closely with their British counterparts in dealing with the money-laundering problem. U.S. federal law enforcement supports the (NCIS's) Financial Intelligence Unit.

The Criminal Justice Act of 1990 (dealing with international cooperation) enhanced the ability of the authorities to deal with money laundering, including providing the power to hold cash being imported to or exported from the United Kingdom for up to two years if a narcotics connection is suspected, with potential for civil forfeiture. More recent 1993 amendments to the Drug Trafficking Offenses Act of 1986 require banks and other institutions to report suspicious transactions. Under the 1986 act, the reporting of suspicious transactions was voluntary—with the warning that any bank officials who failed to report a suspicious transaction could themselves be prosecuted for money laundering. The 1993 act also created new immunities from civil action for bank officials and others who disclose suspicions of money laundering to the NCIS. The act of 1993 incorporated money laundering for all types of criminal offenses. Previously money laundering had been limited to narcotics and terrorism.

Since April 1, 1994, U.K. banks have been required to maintain records of large currency transactions, including the identity of customers engaging in such transactions, and to report the data regularly to a central authority. Such records are maintained for five years. Suspicious transactions are reported to NCIS. The money-laundering regulations of 1993 also require financial institutions to establish procedures for preventing money laundering (e.g., establishment of internal reporting systems, provision of training in the recognition and handling of transactions that appear to be related to money laundering). The United Kingdom uses a "knowingly or suspectingly" standard and has established systems for identifying, tracing, freezing, seizing, and forfeiting narcotics-related assets. But it has only enacted laws for sharing seized narcotics assets with the United States.

Uruguay
(Medium-high.) Uruguay is a significant financial center in South America, with huge foreign deposits, and money launder-

ing is not illegal. U.S. and European law enforcement officials believe that narcotics traffickers launder money here, both in banks and casas de cambio. However, even though Uruguayan banks were recently used for the deposit of illegal funds, the extent of the problem is not known and there is no solid evidence that money laundering is widespread.

It is also not clear what percentage of money-laundering proceeds are owned by local organizations. There is some indication that outside terrorist groups (e.g., the Basque separatist group ETA or Peru's Shining Path or Tupac Amaru) might be using Uruguay to launder money.

Although the Uruguayan government is adamant in its statements about curbing the practice, money laundering is not yet a crime in Uruguay. There are no controls on the amount of currency or gold entering or leaving the country, and Uruguay has not yet addressed the problem of international transportation of illegal source currency and monetary instruments.

This may change, however, as a result of Uruguay's signing of the Ministerial Communiqué on Money Laundering in Buenos Aires in December 1995, in which it agreed to the establishment and implementation of regulations concerning the international transportation of money and instruments across national borders.

Uruguay has been actively participating in OAS ministerial meetings on money laundering, which culminated in the Buenos Aires Ministerial Conference in December 1995. The Uruguayan drug "czar" was recently elected by acclamation to be the president of the OAS Working Group on Strategies to Fight Narcotics Trafficking in the 21st Century. He is also vice-president of UNDCP. Uruguay takes its international role very seriously and intends to not only cooperate, but also to take the lead in the fight against the use and trafficking of illegal narcotics and has cooperated in good faith with the United States on all narcotics-related investigations.

The U.S.-Uruguayan bilateral MLAT became effective in May 1994, and Uruguay ratified the 1988 U.N. Convention in September 1994 and deposited its instruments of ratification in March 1995. Money laundering is still not a criminal offense, although a money-laundering bill, presented to Uruguayan parliament in early 1996, would make it so. Banks and casas de cambio are required to record large currency transactions over U.S.$10,000 and to make their records available quickly to the central bank on request. All financial institutions are required to monitor transactions. The law provides for legal penalties if violations occur, but to date there has been little or no enforcement. Uruguayan law requires that each financial institution keep an accessible database on all transactions exceeding U.S.$10,000 and requires that those making such a transaction identify themselves. Banking officials are held liable if they commit acts considered criminal, or if they approve or overlook actions that entail violations of the law, including those that might involve money laundering.

Nevertheless, money laundering as such is not considered a crime, and the government has not adopted specific due-diligence or banker-negligence laws that would make individual bankers responsible if their institutions launder money, whether or not the transactions are connected with other criminal activity. However, the central bank can revoke the licenses of banks and casas de cambio involved in money laundering.

Central bankers have told U.S. representatives they would support a judicial request for information related to investigations involving money laundering. However, in 1994–1995 a solid investigation involving casas de cambio and banks in the capital, Montevideo, was derailed because of the extraordinary amount of information that Uruguayan courts demanded before approving any request for financial or banking records. Courts in such cases require a level of information normally unavailable to the investigator, thus preventing effective access to banking records.

Uruguay still does not have an established system for identifying, tracing, freezing, seizing, or forfeiting narcotics-related assets. This too is to be addressed with the proposed money-laundering bill. No known legal loopholes exist that will allow launderers to shield assets. Although the government can legally seize laundered drug money from banks or businesses, as far as is known it has never applied the asset seizure law in a case involving a money-laundering-related crime.

Strict bank secrecy laws that protect assets can be lifted by judicial decree to permit access to asset information, but it is rarely done. Although the law allows for criminal forfeiture, the government has never used the law against convicted narcotics traffickers. The courts, sensitive to any violation of rights, must first give such authorization. Still, Uruguay seized the assets of narcotraffickers in a recent operation in the province of Rivera, but it is not clear whether the government will be able to retain those assets.

Uruguay currently lacks any laws for sharing seized narcotics assets with other countries, although existing laws contain a legal basis for establishing potential agreements on sharing. In addition, Uruguay has expressed a willingness to negotiate such an agreement with other countries.

Vanuatu

(Low-medium.) There have been few reports of drug traffickers laundering proceeds in Vanuatu, but the island remains a concern because of its strict bank secrecy, its lack of foreign exchange controls, and the ease of creating offshore shell corporations. An offshore financial center for more than 20 years, Vanuatu has registered more than 100 foreign banks and incorporated more than 1,000 companies, more than 600 of which are considered offshore companies. It is believed that traffickers use these corporations to establish bank accounts in countries other than Vanuatu and then launder money through these foreign banks.

Venezuela

(High.) Venezuela is a major drug money-laundering center because of its proximity to Colombia as well as the size and sophistication of its financial markets. However, Venezuela is not considered a tax haven or an offshore banking center. Rather, Venezuela generally exports capital in the form of capital flight to the United States and other tax havens. Most money laundering occurs through casas de cambio, commercial banks, casinos, fraudulently invoiced foreign trade, contraband, and real estate transactions. Money laundering in Venezuela is closely linked to cocaine trafficking by Colombian organizations. Although the narcotics proceeds are primarily owned by Colombian or other third-country nationals, the money laundering networks are generally run by Venezuelans. Laundering transactions usually involve the exchange of U.S. dollars in cash or monetary instruments (such as postal money orders) for Colombian pesos or Venezuelan bolivares.

Venezuelan government exchange controls were imposed in 1994 to staunch the flow of flight capital occurring during the financial crisis. Although this was not the intent, these policies stimulated the growth of a large illegal parallel exchange market, which created new opportunities for money launderers to exploit. Since July 1995, the government has permitted a legal parallel exchange market to exist through the trading of Brady bonds on the Caracas stock exchange.

The enactment of the 1993 Organic Drug Law was a major step forward in compliance with the 1988 U.N. Convention and other international agreements. The law explicitly criminalized money laundering associated with narcotics trafficking. The law applies to all financial institutions as well as such nonfinancial businesses as real estate brokers. Article 37 of the 1993 Organic Drug Law defines money laundering as a crime with two formulations consistent with the terms of the U.N. Convention.

Money laundering is defined as (a) "hiding or concealing the origin, nature, location, movement, or destination of capital or income, either liquid or fixed, with knowledge of their origin as products of the illicit traffic in drugs, narcotics, and toxic substances," and (b) "transfer or conversion of assets, capital, or other rights, with knowledge that they are products of illicit activities." The law imposes sanctions of 15 to 25 years imprisonment for money-laundering crimes. In addition, the law establishes asset-seizure and forfeiture procedures. Other important aspects of the law include the following:

- Banks and other financial institutions are required to self-initiate reporting of suspicious transactions to the Technical Judicial Police.
- A due-diligence principle is imposed on directors and officers of financial institutions.
- The use of anonymous accounts or fictitious names is prohibited. Complete identification of account holders is required.
- Financial institutions are required to maintain records for five years of all account transactions and to make them available to law enforcement investigators.
- Financial institutions are required to not divulge to account holders when they are under investigation.
- The Superintendency of Banks is required to monitor financial institutions to ensure that they develop adequate internal control policies and to conduct audits to ensure compliance.
- Officers and employees of financial institutions who report suspicious transactions are not subject to civil liability if sued by account holders.
- The central bank of Venezuela is required to design and develop a database on all foreign currency transactions and to provide information on such transactions to the Technical Judicial Police or other law enforcement agencies.

- The Ministry of Justice and the Office of Notaries are required to maintain computerized databases on real estate transactions and to maintain special vigilance over any cash transactions.
- The Ministry of Finance is required to exercise control over trade in precious metals, stones, and jewelry, as well as monitoring the invoicing of export and import transactions and commercial loans that are not considered normal business operations.

Despite the provisions of the 1993 Organic Drug Law, in practice few banks or other financial institutions have complied fully with these requirements. The Venezuelan financial crisis that erupted in 1994 has diverted government attention and resources from enforcing controls on money laundering. Government takeovers of failing banks makes the government increasingly directly responsible for monitoring suspicious transactions, mostly due to the fact that the Venezuelan government now controls about 30 percent of the commercial banking system.

The financial crisis has also led to the negotiation and signing of an MLAT between the United States and Venezuela, to facilitate the exchange of information about illegal banking practices, which may ultimately benefit cooperative anti-money-laundering efforts. Venezuela and the United States signed a Kerry amendment agreement in November 1990 for the exchange of information on cash transactions in excess of U.S.$10,000. The agreement was put into effect by Central Bank Resolution No. 90-12-05. However, the agreement applies only to transactions in foreign currencies, including the U.S. dollar; it does not cover cash transactions in Venezuelan bolivares.

Venezuelan police agencies have initiated investigations and enforcement actions against several major money-laundering organizations under the 1993 Organic Drug Law, but these cases have been frustrated by the courts. In October 1993, the Venezuelan National Guard successfully dismantled the Sinforoso Caballero money-laundering organization, which operated on the Colombian border with links to the Cali cartel. Subsequent investigations revealed that a multinational financial group acted as the international connection for this money-laundering organization. Indictments were issued by a Caracas criminal court judge against 34 individuals. However, because of pressure on the judicial system by the defendants, jurisdiction in the case was changed to the state of Tachira, where most of the defendants resided. In May 1994, the Tachira judge dismissed the arrest warrants against all defendants in the case. Although the Venezuelan supreme court overturned this decision in December 1994, no action has been taken to reopen the case.

In 1995, the Venezuelan congress began consideration of two key pieces of legislation that will have important implications for controlling money laundering. The first is the Casinos Bill, which would impose cash-transaction-reporting requirements on casinos, as well as tightening up law enforcement oversight of gambling activities. The second is the Organized Crime Bill, which would introduce conspiracy provisions into Venezuelan criminal law.

Vietnam

(Low.) Vietnam currently offers few attractions to drug money launderers, but that situation could change as foreign banks open branches. The Vietnamese are known to engage in heroin trafficking, and Australian officials report incidents of Vietnamese nationals smuggling gold between Australia and Vietnam, which they believe is related to heroin trafficking. It is believed that payment for some heroin shipments to Australia has been made by wire transfers from Australia to the United States. In 1995, the Vietnamese government began consideration of drug-trafficking controls, and U.S. officials have repeatedly urged the Vietnamese to consider incorporation of FATF's 40 money-laundering countermeasures.

Yemen

(No priority.) There are no statistics indicating that there is money laundering in Yemen.

Yugoslavia

(Low.) In Yugoslavia, now composed of only Serbia and Montenegro, laundering of drug money has been reported anecdotally, but persuasive evidence is lacking. There are no specific laws prohibiting money laundering. If the practice occurs, it is probably limited. Belgrade is not an important financial center, a tax haven, nor an offshore banking center. Belgrade's financial system is primitive in comparison with Western European capitals.

Given the insolvency of local banks and their complete inability to effect rapid electronic transfers, banks would be an unlikely vehicle for laundering large sums of money. Furthermore, with the scandals that have rocked the banking system over the past several years, including the freezing of more than U.S.$4 billion in hard-currency savings deposits, there are factors that would discourage anyone, drug traffickers included, from depositing large sums in local banks. Banking authorities in Yugoslavia here point to Cyprus and Switzerland as more likely candidates for money laundering by Yugoslavian nationals.

Belgrade, however, does harbor organized criminal elements, which are known to be active in drug trafficking. Because of U.N. sanctions, organized crime was, and still is, heavily involved in the smuggling of prohibited strategic materials—principally oil and oil products. With the suspension of some U.N. sanctions in late November 1995, and the legalization of imports of oil and fuel, organized crime has sought more profitable alternatives, including both drugs and arms.

Zambia

(Low.) The Bank of Zambia and the Zambian Drug Enforcement Commission (DEC) are increasingly concerned that money laundering is rampant in the banking industry. They have proposed tightening banking standards through legislative action. The government publicly denounces drug trafficking and supports the ongoing efforts of the autonomous DEC. The DEC has used strengthened narcotics laws this year to confiscate the property of traffickers. The head of the DEC collaborates with his counterparts in the region to improve regional antitrafficking efforts. (Zambia ratified the 1988 U.N. Convention in 1993.) The DEC has increasingly used its legal authority to confiscate property of suspected drug traffickers and money launderers; however, the courts have not always sustained these confiscations.

The DEC and the Ministry of Legal Affairs cooperate with their counterparts in the Southern African Development Council. The DEC has received training from British antinarcotics teams and works closely with its British counterparts, as well as having received limited assistance from Germany, South Africa, and the United States. Zambia's antinarcotics master plan was developed in cooperation with the U.N.'s drug-control program.

The Zambian Anti-Corruption Commission investigates allegations of corruption, some of which have touched even government ministers. Such allegations have never been fully proven to the satisfaction of President Chiluba, but led to the resignation of then Foreign Minister Vernon Mwaanga in January 1994. (Mwaanga remains, all the same, an important officer in the ruling Movement for Multi-Party Democracy Party.) Recently, corruption allegations have focused on embezzling state funds and not on narcotics-related corruption. It is alleged that drug traffickers are taking advantage of the weak enforcement of banking laws and laundering drug money in a number of banks and foreign exchange houses.

No legal proceedings have yet been directed against the allegedly corrupt financial institutions or the government officials who have financial interests in those banks or foreign exchange houses.

Zimbabwe
(No priority.) Zimbabwe's currency regulations continue to make it a less than ideal place for money laundering. An asset forfeiture act was passed in 1990 but remains underused, since both the judiciary and law enforcement seem to lack an understanding of its application.

SUMMARY

The Future of
Money Laundering

As we have seen, in recent years crime has become increasingly international in scope, and the financial aspects of crime are complex as a result of the rapidly changing advances in technology. International organized crime is an enormous and multifaceted problem. It is not only a law enforcement problem but a national and international security threat as well.

Many countries around the world already engage in concerted efforts to combat international organized crime. Through the enactment of counter-money-laundering laws, bilateral and multilateral agreements, and other cooperative efforts, nations have joined together to foster an international awareness of the seriousness and threat of organized crime and to acknowledge this problem directly. An increasing number of countries have moved to deny criminal enterprises unfettered access to their financial systems. Although much progress has been made, and despite all these efforts, there are still nations that have not yet adequately addressed this problem. And the international criminal is taking full advantage, moving vast sums of illicit money through the world's financial systems. International criminals know no geographic boundaries and can still find safe havens in which to hide.

If the United States, along with its international partners and allies, are ultimately going to be successful in this fight, then it must make it even more difficult for criminals. Efforts must focus upon those areas where the criminals are now going and foster cooperation, one way or another, with those nations that, heretofore, have allowed criminal enterprise to flourish unchecked.

The president of the United States, during his address to the United Nations on October 22, 1995, authorized a number of actions that provide an even more aggressive approach to dealing with international criminal organizations. Those countries in which these organizations are now allowed to operate and prosper, unrestricted by counter-money-laundering efforts, will be compelled to conform to the international goals established to deal with the issue of international crime. These countries will be held publicly accountable for their role in the common effort to deter international criminal activities. To implement his goals, the president is assigning high priority to negotiating agreements that ensure governments' compliance with internationally accepted anti-money-laundering standards. The Department of the Treasury is coordinating this initiative and working with the Departments of State and Justice, the bank regulators, and the intelligence community to expedite this process.

With few exceptions, criminals are motivated by one thing—profit. Greed drives the criminal, and the end result is that illegally gained money must be introduced into a nation's legitimate financial system. Money laundering involves disguising assets so they can be used without detection of the illegal activity that produced them. The success, therefore, of organized crime is based upon its ability to launder money. Through money laundering, the criminal transforms the monetary proceeds derived from criminal activity into funds with a seemingly legal source.

This process has devastating social consequences. For one thing, money laundering provides the fuel for drug dealers, terrorists, arms dealers, and other criminals to operate and expand their operations. Criminals manipulate financial systems in the United States and abroad to further a wide range of illicit activities. Left unchecked, money laundering can erode the integrity of the world's financial institutions.

The profits of crime that creep into the financial systems of the United States and other nations are staggering. As previously noted, in the United States alone, estimates of the amount of drug profits moving through the financial system have been as high as $100 billion. Consider the fact that money laundering extends far beyond hiding narcotics profits, to include monies tied to crimes ranging from tax fraud to terrorism. Plus, arms smuggling adds many additional billions of dollars to the criminals' profits. Criminal activities, without restraint, fundamentally destabilize political and economic reform. As history demonstrates again and again, political stability, democracy, and free markets depend on solvent, stable, and honest financial, commercial, and trade systems.

There is now worldwide recognition that nations must deal firmly and effectively with increasingly elusive, well-financed, and technologically adept criminal organizations. These organizations are determined to use every means available to subvert the financial systems that are the cornerstone of legitimate international commerce. As organized crime develops economic power, it corrupts democratic institutions and undermines free enterprise. Money laundering, correctly, is now being viewed as the central dilemma in dealing with all forms of international organized crime because financial gain means power. Organized crime is assuming an increasingly significant role that threatens the safety and security of peoples, states, and democratic institutions.

Be it through the G-7-sponsored Financial Action Task Force, the various Financial Intelligence Units, Interpol, or the more diplomatic offices of organizations such as the Summit of the Americas, the United Nations, the Asia Pacific Economic Council, or the European Union, all efforts should be directed toward implementing and directing efforts devoted to combating international organized crime. As a whole, the organizations should strive to advance counter-money-laundering measures through prevention, detection, and enforcement of financial crime, as well as other international criminal activity.

Thoughtful efforts should be undertaken to facilitate information sharing and coordination among nations in worldwide criminal investigative matters. To date, the adoption of major money laundering resolutions by various countries illustrate a common commitment to thwarting international financial crimes and their desire to strengthen international cooperation. Still, there is unresolved ambiguity among the nations themselves, and future efforts should direct themselves to international codification of four central issues:

1. Provide for the criminal prosecution of persons who knowingly participate in the laundering of proceeds derived from serious criminal activity.
2. Allow for the seizure of property, with sufficient legal investigative authority for law enforcement officials to identify, trace, and freeze assets derived from illicit activities; allow for reporting of unusual or suspect currency or other transactions by banks and other financial institutions to appropriate officials who would have authority to conduct further investigative inquiries.

3. Require financial institutions to maintain, at least for five years after the conclusion of the transaction, all necessary records on transactions, both domestic and international, to enable member countries to properly investigate money laundering and to enhance international cooperation by enabling signatory countries to respond to requests from authorities in other countries for such records.
4. Allow for the expeditious extradition of individuals charged with money-laundering offenses.

In the main, international communication and the sharing of financial intelligence information are the keys to addressing the global problem of money laundering. This amounts to a shared dedication, if you will, to ignore the realities of political pressure and to embrace the wholesale promotion of effective anti-money-laundering controls.

Admittedly, this will not be a stagnant process in light of constantly changing money-laundering methods and the emergence of new technologies and services within the financial services sector. But with commitment, attention to detail, and, most important, dialogue, the partnerships that are essential to combating money laundering and financial crime will bridge private and governmental sectors and force attention to the problem outside of the narrow bureaucratic thinking of the past and into the light of public scrutiny.

Money laundering and international narcotics trafficking will be forever linked. Will narcotics disappear from the global stage? No. Will money laundering? Not as long as narcotics trafficking and other high-profit crimes continue to generate such exorbitant revenues. It is a world unto itself. A business complete with budgets, losses, and profit margins. It is both an art and a science . . . the commerce of choice in the shadow world of criminal enterprise.

APPENDIX

Forty Recommendations of the G-7 Financial Action Task Force on Money Laundering

- The Financial Action Task Force on Money Laundering (FATF) is an intergovernmental body whose purpose is the development and promotion of policies to combat money laundering—the processing of criminal proceeds in order to disguise their illegal origin. These policies aim to prevent such proceeds from being utilized in future criminal activities and from affecting legitimate economic activities.

- FATF currently consists of 26 countries and two international organizations. Its membership includes the major financial center countries of Europe, North America, and Asia. It is a multidisciplinary body—as is essential in dealing with money laundering—bringing together the policy-making power of legal, financial, and law enforcement experts. (NOTE: References in this document to "countries" should be taken to apply equally to "territories" or "jurisdictions." The 26 FATF member countries and governments are Australia, Austria, Belgium, Canada, Denmark, Finland, France, Germany, Greece, Hong Kong, Iceland, Ireland, Italy, Japan, Luxembourg, the Kingdom of the Netherlands, New Zealand, Norway, Portugal, Singapore, Spain, Sweden, Switzerland, Turkey, the United Kingdom, and the United States. The two international organizations are the European Commission and the Gulf Cooperation Council.

- This need to cover all relevant aspects of the fight against money laundering is reflected in the scope of the 40 FATF recommendations—the measures that the task force has agreed to implement and which all countries are encouraged to adopt. The recommendations were originally drawn up in 1990. In 1996 the 40 recommendations were revised to take into account the experience gained over the last six years and to reflect the changes that have occurred in the money-laundering problem.

- These 40 recommendations set out the basic framework for anti-money-laundering efforts, and they are designed to be of universal application. They cover the criminal justice system and law enforcement, the financial system and its regulation, and international cooperation.

- It was recognized from the outset of the FATF that countries have diverse legal and financial systems, and so all cannot take identical measures. The recommendations are therefore the principles for action in this field, for countries to implement according to their particular circumstances and constitutional frameworks, allowing countries a measure of flexibility rather than prescribing every detail. The measures are not particularly complex or difficult, provided there is the political will to act. Nor do they compromise the freedom to engage in legitimate transactions or threaten economic development.

- FATF countries are clearly committed to accept the discipline of being subjected to multilateral surveillance and peer review. All member countries have their implementation of the 40 recommendations monitored through a two-pronged approach: an annual self-assessment exercise and the more detailed mutual evaluation process under which each member country is subject to an on-site examination by G-7 representatives. In addition, the FATF carries out cross-country reviews of measures taken to implement particular recommendations.
- These measures are essential for the creation of an effective anti-money-laundering framework.

(General Framework of the Recommendations)
1. Each country should take immediate steps to ratify and to implement fully the 1988 United Nations Convention against Illicit Traffic in Narcotic Drugs and Psychotropic Substances (the Vienna Convention).
2. Financial institution secrecy laws should be conceived so as not to inhibit implementation of these recommendations.
3. An effective money-laundering enforcement program should include increased multilateral cooperation and mutual legal assistance in money-laundering investigations and prosecutions and extradition in money-laundering cases, where possible.

(Role of National Legal Systems in Combating Money Laundering)
4. Each country should take such measures as may be necessary, including legislative ones, to enable it to criminalize money laundering as set forth in the Vienna Convention. Each country should extend the offense of drug money laundering to one based on serious offenses. Each country would determine which serious crimes would be designated as money laundering predicate offenses.

5. As provided in the Vienna Convention, the offense of money laundering should apply at least to knowing of money-laundering activity, including the concept that knowledge may be inferred from objective factual circumstances.

6. Where possible, corporations themselves—not only their employees—should be subject to criminal liability.

7. Countries should adopt measures similar to those set forth in the Vienna Convention as may be necessary, including legislative ones, to enable their competent authorities to confiscate property laundered, proceeds from, instrumentalities used in or intended for use in the commission of any money-laundering offense, or property of corresponding value, without prejudicing the rights of bona fide third parties.

    Such measures should include the authority to (1) identify, trace, and evaluate property that is subject to confiscation; (2) carry out provisional measures, such as freezing and seizing, to prevent any dealing, transferring, or disposing of such property; and (3) take any appropriate investigative measures.

    In addition to confiscation and criminal sanctions, countries also should consider monetary and civil penalties and/or proceedings, including civil proceedings, to void contracts entered into by parties, where parties knew or should have known that as a result of the contract, the State would be prejudiced in its ability to recover financial claims, e.g., through confiscation or collection of fines and penalties.

(Role of the Financial System in Combating Money Laundering)

8. Recommendations 10 to 29 should apply not only to banks, but also to nonbank financial institutions. Even for those nonbank financial institutions that are not subject to a formal prudential supervisory regime in all countries (e.g.,

bureaux de change), governments should ensure that these institutions are subject to the same anti-money-laundering laws or regulations as all other financial institutions and that these laws or regulations are implemented effectively.

9. The appropriate national authorities should consider applying recommendations 10 through 21 and 23 to the conduct of financial activities as a commercial undertaking by businesses or professions that are not financial institutions, where such conduct is allowed or not prohibited. It is left to each country to decide whether special situations should be defined where the application of anti-money-laundering measures is not necessary, e.g., when a financial activity is carried out on an occasional or limited basis.

10. Financial institutions should not keep anonymous accounts or accounts in obviously fictitious names: they should be required (by law, by regulations, by agreements between supervisory authorities and financial institutions, or by self-regulatory agreements among financial institutions) to identify on the basis of an official or other reliable identifying document and to record the identity of their clients, either occasional or usual, when establishing business relations or conducting transactions (in particular opening of accounts or passbooks, entering into fiduciary transactions, renting of safe-deposit boxes, or performing large cash transactions).

To fulfill identification requirements concerning legal entities, financial institutions should, when necessary, take measures to:

   A. verify the legal existence and structure of the customer by obtaining, either from a public register or from the customer or both, proof of incorporation, including information concerning the customer's name, legal form, address, directors, and provisions regulating the power to bind the entity, and

B. verify that any person purporting to act on behalf
of the customer is so authorized and identify that
person.

11. Financial institutions should take reasonable measures to
obtain information about the true identity of the persons
on whose behalf an account is opened or a transaction
conducted if there are any doubts as to whether these
clients or customers are acting on their own behalf, for
example, in the case of domiciliary companies (i.e., institutions, corporations, foundations, or trusts that do not
conduct any commercial or manufacturing business or any
other form of commercial operation in the country where
their registered office is located).

12. Financial institutions should maintain, for at least five
years, all necessary records on transactions, both domestic
and international, to enable them to comply swiftly with
information requests from the competent authorities.
Such records must be sufficient to permit reconstruction
of individual transactions (including the amounts and
types of currency involved, if any) so as to provide, if necessary, evidence for prosecution of criminal behavior.

Financial institutions should keep records on customer identification (e.g., copies or records of such official
identification documents as passports, identity cards, or
driver's licenses), account files, and business correspon-
dence for at least five years after the account is closed.

These documents should be available to domestic
competent authorities in the context of relevant criminal
prosecutions and investigations.

13. Countries should pay special attention to money-laundering threats inherent in new or developing technologies
that might favor anonymity, and take measures, if needed,
to prevent their use in money-laundering schemes.

14. Financial institutions should pay special attention to all complex, large transactions and all unusual patterns of transactions that have no apparent economic or visible lawful purpose. The background and purpose of such transactions should, as far as possible, be examined, the findings established in writing, and be made available to help supervisors, auditors, and law enforcement agencies.

15. If financial institutions suspect that funds stem from a criminal activity, they should be required to report promptly their suspicions to the competent authorities.

16. Financial institutions, their directors, officers, and employees should be protected by legal provisions from criminal or civil liability for breach of any restriction on disclosure of information imposed by contract or by any legislative, regulatory, or administrative provision if they report their suspicions in good faith to the competent authorities, even if they did not know precisely what the underlying criminal activity was and regardless of whether illegal activity actually occurred.

17. Financial institutions, their directors, officers, and employees should not—or, where appropriate, should not be allowed to—warn their customers when information relating to them is being reported to the competent authorities.

18. Financial institutions reporting their suspicions should comply with instructions from the competent authorities.

19. Financial institutions should develop programs against money laundering. These programs should include, as a minimum:

   A. the development of internal policies, procedures, and controls, including the designation of compliance officers at management level and adequate screening procedures to ensure high standards when hiring employees;

   B. an ongoing employee training program;

   C. an audit function to test the system.

20. Financial institutions should ensure that the principles mentioned above are also applied to branches and majority-owned subsidiaries located abroad, especially in countries that do not, or insufficiently, apply these recommendations, to the extent that local applicable laws and regulations permit. When local applicable laws and regulations prohibit this implementation, competent authorities in the country of the mother institution should be informed by the financial institutions that they cannot apply these recommendations.

21. Financial institutions should give special attention to business relations and transactions with persons, including companies and financial institutions, from countries that do not, or insufficiently, apply these recommendations. Whenever these transactions have no apparent economic or visible lawful purpose, their background and purpose should, as far as possible, be examined, and the findings established in writing and be made available to help supervisors, auditors, and law enforcement agencies.

22. Countries should consider implementing feasible measures to detect or monitor the physical cross-border transportation of cash and bearer negotiable instruments, subject to strict safeguards to ensure proper use of information and without impeding in any way the freedom of capital movements.

23. Countries should consider the feasibility and utility of a system where banks and other financial institutions and intermediaries would report all domestic and international currency transactions above a fixed amount to a national central agency with a computerized database, available to competent authorities for use in money-laundering cases, subject to strict safeguards to ensure proper use of the information.

24. Countries should further encourage in general the development of modern and secure techniques of money man-

agement, including increased use of checks, payment cards, direct deposit of salary checks, and book entry recording of securities, as a means to encourage the replacement of cash transfers.

25. Countries should take notice of the potential for abuse of shell corporations by money launderers and should consider whether additional measures are required to prevent unlawful use of such entities.

26. The competent authorities supervising banks or other financial institutions or intermediaries, or other competent authorities, should ensure that the supervised institutions have adequate programs to guard against money laundering. These authorities should cooperate and lend expertise spontaneously or on request with other domestic judicial or law enforcement authorities in money-laundering investigations and prosecutions.

27. Competent authorities should be designated to ensure an effective implementation of all these recommendations through administrative supervision and regulation in other professions dealing with cash as defined by each country.

28. The competent authorities should establish guidelines that will assist financial institutions in detecting suspicious patterns of behavior by their customers. It is understood that such guidelines must develop over time and will never be exhaustive. It is further understood that such guidelines will primarily serve as an educational tool for financial institutions' personnel.

29. The competent authorities regulating or supervising financial institutions should take the necessary legal or regulatory measures to guard against control or acquisition of a significant participation in financial institutions by criminals or their confederates.

(Strengthening of International Cooperation)

30. National administrations should consider recording, at least in the aggregate, international flows of cash in whatever currency so that estimates can be made of cash flows and reflows from various sources abroad, when this is combined with central bank information. Such information should be made available to the International Monetary Fund and the Bank for International Settlements to facilitate international studies.

31. International competent authorities, perhaps Interpol and the World Customs Organization, should be given responsibility for gathering and disseminating information to competent authorities about the latest developments in money laundering and money-laundering techniques. Central banks and bank regulators could do the same on their network. National authorities in various spheres, in consultation with trade associations, could then disseminate this to financial institutions in individual countries.

32. Each country should make efforts to improve a spontaneous or "upon request" international information exchange relating to suspicious transactions, persons, and corporations involved in those transactions between competent authorities. Strict safeguards should be established to ensure that this exchange of information is consistent with national and international provisions on privacy and data protection.

(Other Forms of Cooperation)

33. Countries should try to ensure on a bilateral or multilateral basis that different knowledge standards in national definitions—i.e., different standards concerning the intentional element of the infraction—do not affect the ability or willingness of countries to provide each other with mutual legal assistance.

34. International cooperation should be supported by a network of bilateral and multilateral agreements and arrangements based on generally shared legal concepts with the aim of providing practical measures to affect the widest possible range of mutual assistance.

35. Countries should be encouraged to ratify and implement relevant international conventions on money laundering such as the 1990 Council of Europe Convention on Laundering, Search, Seizure, and Confiscation of the Proceeds from Crime.

36. Cooperative investigations among countries' appropriate competent authorities should be encouraged. One valid and effective investigative technique in this respect is controlled delivery related to assets known or suspected to be the proceeds of crime. Countries are encouraged to support this technique, where possible.

37. There should be procedures for mutual assistance in criminal matters regarding the use of compulsory measures, including the production of records by financial institutions and other persons, the search of persons and premises, seizure and obtaining of evidence for use in money-laundering investigations and prosecutions and in related actions in foreign jurisdictions.

38. There should be authority to take expeditious action in response to requests by foreign countries to identify, freeze, seize, and confiscate proceeds or other property of corresponding value to such proceeds, based on money laundering or the crimes underlying the laundering activity. There should also be arrangements for coordinating seizure and confiscation proceedings that may include the sharing of confiscated assets.

39. To avoid conflicts of jurisdiction, consideration should be given to devising and applying mechanisms for determining the best venue for prosecution of defendants in the interests of justice in cases that are subject to pros-

ecution in more than one country. Similarly, there should be arrangements for coordinating seizure and confiscation proceedings, which may include the sharing of confiscated assets.

40. Countries should have procedures in place to extradite, where possible, individuals charged with a money-laundering offense or related offenses. With respect to its national legal system, each country should recognize money laundering as an extraditable offense. Subject to their legal frameworks, countries may consider simplifying extradition by allowing direct transmission of extradition requests between appropriate ministries, extraditing persons based only on warrants of arrests or judgments, extraditing their nationals, and/or introducing a simplified extradition of consenting persons who waive formal extradition proceedings.

GLOSSARY

Selected Acronyms
Used in the Text

BSA: International Bank Security Association

CARICOM: Caribbean Community Secretariat

CFATF: Caribbean Financial Action Task Force

CFZ: Colon Free Zone (Panama)

CICAD: Inter-American Drug Abuse Control Commission (OAS)

CMIR: A report of international transaction or currency or monetary instruments (a U.S. Customs form)

CRI: Centrale Recherche Informatiedienst (Central Intelligence Investigation Service, the Netherlands)

CTR: Currency Transaction Report (U.S. IRS form)

DEC: Drug Enforcement Commission (Zambia)

DNCD: National Drug Control Directorate (Dominican Republic)

EU: European Union

FATF: Financial Action Task Force

FAU: financial analysis unit

FIEA: financial information exchange agreement

FinCEN: Financial Crimes Enforcement Network

FIU: financial information unit

FOPAC: Proceeds of Crime Group (Interpol)

FSA: Freedom Support Act

IBC: international business company

IBSA: International Bank Security Association

INCSR: International Narcotics Control Strategy Report

INL/ICJ: International Narcotics and Law Enforcement Affairs, Office of International Criminal Justice (U.S. State Department)

MLAT: mutual legal assistance treaty

MMD: Movement for Multi-Party Democracy (Zambia)

MOT: Meldpunkt Ongebruikelijke Transacties (Transaction Disclosure Office, the Netherlands)

NCIS: (United Kingdom)

NDDCB: National Dangerous Drugs Control Board (Sri Lanka)

NDLEA: National Drug Law Enforcement Authority (Nigeria)

NIS: newly independent states (ex-Soviet Union)

OAS: Organization of American States

OCDETF: organized crime drug enforcement task force

OGBS: Offshore Group of Banking Supervisors

ONCB: Office of the Narcotics Control Board

PGR: (Argentina)

PTJ: Technical Judicial Police (Panama)

SEED: Support for Eastern European Democracies

SWIFT: Society for Worldwide Interbank Financial Telecommunications

UAE: United Arab Emirates

UNDCP: United Nations Drug Control Program

ABOUT THE AUTHOR

Brett F. Woods is an inspector general for the state of New Mexico. He is a certified government financial manager and a certified fraud examiner and currently serves as the president of the New Mexico Chapter of the National Association of Government Accountants. A Vietnam veteran of the U.S. Army Special Forces and former special agent with the U.S. Secret Service, Mr. Woods holds a bachelor of science degree in police science and a master of public administration degree and is the author of numerous articles and books related to the field. His professional affiliations include the International Association of Chiefs of Police, the International Narcotics Officers Association, and the Southwest Intergovernmental Audit Forum. His first Paladin book was *E-Money: Financial Management in the Electronic Age.*